The Crime Buff's Guide to Outlaw Texas

Ron Franscell

gpp

Guilford, Connecticut

To buy books in quantity for corporate use
or incentives, call **(800) 962-0973**
or e-mail **premiums@GlobePequot.com**.

Text design: Sheryl P. Kober
Layout: Joanna Beyer
Project editor: John Burbidge
Maps: Sue Murray © Morris Book Publishing, LLC
All photos by Ron Franscell unless otherwise noted.

Library of Congress Cataloging-in-Publication data is available on file.

ISBN 978-0-7627-5965-1

Printed in the United States of America
10 9 8 7 6 5 4 3 2 1

To Mary
Who is always there

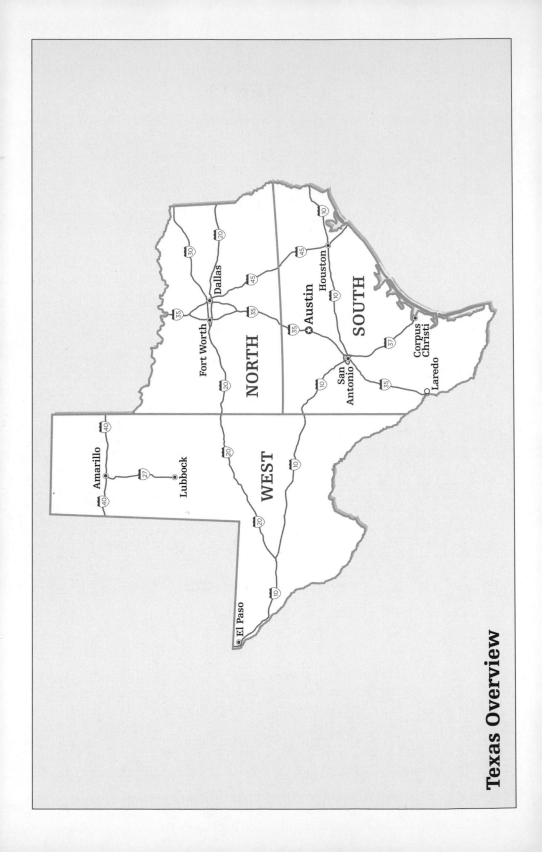

Texas Overview

CONTENTS

History is merely a list of surprises.
It can only prepare us to be surprised yet again.

—KURT VONNEGUT

INTRODUCTION:
CHASING SHADOWS

One late November day, back when many more things were black-and-white, I watched the black-and-white newsreels on a neighbor's television. I was six, and I truly didn't understand what it meant when they said the president had been murdered in Dallas.

I am still haunted by those images. I know now, almost fifty years later, what I could not see. The man in the window above. The crimson spray of blood. The fear my mother must have felt. In my mind, this momentous event had played out on a great stage, larger than I could ever see, as all consequential and inexplicable moments in human history must.

To most Americans born after 1963, John F. Kennedy is merely the name of a man who has always been dead, a ghost haunting history books. Dealey Plaza is merely a place where something terrible happened a long time ago, behind the gauzy veil of the past, not in all the violent colors of our collective grief.

So when I actually visited Dealey Plaza for the first time, as a forty-something father, I found it to be much smaller, much more intimate than my childhood imagination had built it. Peering down from a sixth-floor window of the Texas School Book Depository, the fatal shots no longer seemed especially distant, certainly nothing that required a military sharpshooter. To me, they were shots that any twelve-year-old Wyoming kid who'd ever hunted rabbits could make.

Through this window I saw it all below, as if I had unwittingly stepped into a wrinkle of time where I could see forward and back, in color and black-and-white at the same moment.

Being there changed everything.

I have since felt the same unexpected intimacy at Ford's Theatre, the Oklahoma City bombing memorial, Antietam's Bloody Lane, and the Alamo—all places where imagination, myth, and history entangle. Places where the past exists just beneath the surface of the present. Places best seen through a haunted, magical window.

Through that window, I saw a black spider on hit man (and alleged JFK assassin) Mac Wallace's headstone. I felt the magnetic pull of slain Tejano singer Selena, whose memorial statue on Corpus Christi's seawall is seldom without visitors. I heard jukebox music and laughter in the decaying ruins of "the best little whorehouse in Texas." And I was moved by mere scratches in stone . . . the faces of killer Andrea Yates's five children etched in their tombstone, or the simple X that marks the graves of executed killers in Peckerwood Hill, Huntsville's prison cemetery.

Let this book be your window. Our appreciation of history begins in the places where it happened. And now the magic of GPS (Global Positioning System) allows you to stand in a precise historic spot, as best as our modern technology and imaginations can muster. We have made every attempt to put you literally within inches of the past. History is how we know, how we learn. And being there makes all the difference.

Ron Franscell
San Antonio, Texas

HOW TO USE THIS BOOK

The entries in this book are divided into five chapters: three geographic regions (South, North, and West Texas) and two segments, one about outlaws Bonnie and Clyde and the other about the tragic assassination of John F. Kennedy. Each entry has physical and GPS directions that will let you stand in the footsteps of history—not in the general vicinity, but literally on a spot relevant to one of Texas's most notable and fascinating crimes or outlaw-related figures.

Crimes big and small have been committed every single day since mankind began to distinguish right from wrong. This book cannot begin to aggregate every injustice, every crime, every inhumanity ever visited upon the space we now call Texas, although even the smallest crime certainly affects victims, survivors, and communities as much as the most celebrated crimes in our history. And in some cases here, I have chosen only a few representative sites. So please don't be offended if you feel I've overlooked a crime or site you believe should have been included.

A word of warning: Many of these sites are on private land. Always seek permission before venturing onto private property. Do not trespass. It's rude, illegal, and this is Texas, where everybody owns a gun.

I made every effort to be precise in my facts and directions, but being human, I am bound to have erred here and there. If you believe I should include a certain crime in future editions—or if you see an error that should be corrected—please send me a note at Ron Franscell / OUTLAW TEXAS, c/o Globe Pequot Press, 246 Goose Lane, P.O. Box 480, Guilford, CT 06437; or email editorial@globepequot.com.

A NOTE ABOUT GPS ACCURACY

GPS readings are affected by many things, including satellite positions, noise in the radio signal, weather, natural barriers to the signal, and variations between devices. Noise—static, interference, or competing frequencies—can cause errors up to 30 feet. Clouds, bad weather, mountains, or buildings can also skew readings up to 100 feet.

While I've tried to make every GPS coordinate in *The Crime Buff's Guide to Outlaw Texas* as precise as possible, I can't be sure you'll visit under the same conditions. The best possible way to get an accurate reading is to be sure the satellites and your receiver have a clear view of each other, with no clouds, trees, or other interference. If your device doesn't bring you to the right spot, look around. It's likely within a few paces.

1

SOUTH TEXAS

LAWMAN DALLAS STOUDENMIRE'S GRAVE
Alleyton

From I-10 take exit 698 and travel about 1.5 miles down Alleyton Road on the south side of the freeway. The cemetery is on the right. GPS: 29.70828 / -96.48198

Dallas Stoudenmire (1845–1882) was a contemporary of Bat Masterson, Wyatt Earp, and Bill Tilghman—and was involved in more deadly gunfights than all of them put together—but he never reached their mythic status. As a Texas Ranger, a town marshal in El Paso, and a deputy U.S. marshal, the dapper, 6-foot-2 Stoudenmire kept the peace with two six-guns he was quick to draw, especially when drunk.

In 1881, after only three days in his new job as El Paso's town marshal, Stoudenmire stepped into Old West history when he won the infamous "Four Dead in Five Seconds" gunfight. Although he survived several assassination attempts and continued to add to his considerable body count, Stoudenmire was gunned down at age thirty-seven by two old foes. His wife shipped his body back to Alleyton for a funeral funded by the local Masonic lodge, which shelled out $11.55 for Stoudenmire's burial suit and $4.50 for the wood to build his coffin.

GRAVE OF WIFE-KILLER WILLIAM ROE
Anderson

Odd Fellows Cemetery is just south of FM 149, west of Anderson. Likely GPS: 30.48814 / -96.00517

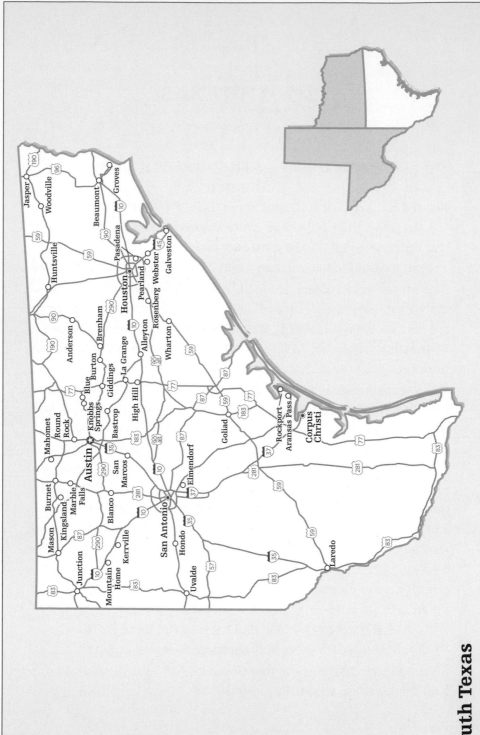

South Texas

Former Huntsville town marshal and deputy sheriff William H. Roe (1856–1888) was convicted and executed for poisoning his wife, Jennie, in 1886 by lacing her coffee with strychnine. Although many vigilantes wanted to lynch him, Roe was legally hanged two years later—the only execution in Grimes County history—and buried in an unmarked grave, likely in the Roe family plot. Historians believe Roe was the first lawman to be legally executed in Texas.

VICTIM MINNIE GOTTHARDT'S GRAVE
Aransas Pass

Prairie View Cemetery is on the east side of FM 1069, just south of TX 35. The grave is in Section 171, Lot 3, Site 5. GPS: 27.91672 / -97.18169

"Big Minnie" Gotthardt (1909–1937) was rumored to be pregnant with serial killer Joe Ball's child when he shot her in the head and buried her in a shallow grave in nearby Ingleside. Although this waitress was described by her customers as "a bossy, displeasing, and obnoxious person," Big Minnie was having an affair with her boss, sadistic tavern owner Joe Ball, when she disappeared—shortly after Joe took a shine to another woman.

Months later, when the cops came to question Ball about several missing waitresses (and possibly feeding them to the pet alligators he kept behind his Elmendorf saloon), he committed suicide. But his helpful handyman, who helped Ball kill and bury at least two waitresses, eventually led police to Minnie's secret grave on the beach. The grisly exhumation of her decaying corpse attracted so many curious bystanders that at least one enterprising local merchant set up a cold-drink stand for them.

Also see "Serial Killer Joe Ball's Grave and Tavern" (Elmendorf), "Victim Hazel Brown's Grave" (Knobbs Springs), and "Ranger Johnny Klevenhagen's Grave" (San Antonio).

TEXAS TOWER
Austin

The University of Texas Main Building is at 2400 Inner Campus Drive, on the western edge of the downtown campus. Guided tours are the only way to see the observation deck, but schedules change constantly; tickets must be purchased (877-475-6633). GPS: 30.286089 / -97.739316

Designed by Paul Philippe Cret, the Spanish Colonial tower atop the University of Texas's Main Building opened in 1937 as Austin's first skyscraper. On top of the limestone tower is a carillon of fifty-six bells, on which songs are played Mondays, Wednesdays, and Fridays by a local carillonneur (this wag is also known to play a death march during final-exam week). But this capital city landmark is not known primarily for its music.

Until the 2007 Virginia Tech rampage, the Texas Tower massacre was the second-deadliest school massacre in U.S. history, right behind Andrew Kehoe's 1927 Michigan school bombing, which killed forty-four innocents.

On August 1, 1966, the modern era of American mass murder exploded to a new height. A twenty-five-year-old architectural engineering student named Charles Whitman (1941–1966) barricaded himself on the observation deck of this 307-foot tower with an enormous arsenal of weapons and ammunition. For the next ninety-six minutes, Whitman—who'd already murdered his wife and mother—fired freely on people below. By the time two policemen finally killed Whitman, sixteen innocent people had died and thirty-one were wounded. In 2001 a Fort Worth man died from complications of a wound inflicted by Whitman, bringing Whitman's official death toll to seventeen. Whitman was shot dead in the northwest corner of the observation deck, over a drainage grate.

A potent symbol of the University of Texas and site of one of the Lone Star State's most harrowing crimes

During the shooting spree, lawmen and trigger-happy citizens alike fired back at Whitman's nearly impenetrable perch. A police sniper was sent aloft in an airplane, but Whitman drove them away with his gunfire. For many years the tower bore the pockmarks where bullets had hit, but they have all been repaired. If you look closely, though, you can still see where the divots were patched.

The coroner later found a small tumor in the ex-marine's brain, but it's impossible to know if it contributed to his crime any more than his dysfunctional childhood. Whitman was eventually buried with his mother—his first victim at The Penthouse, 1212 Guadalupe Street, Apt. 505 (GPS: 30.275916 / -97.743875)—in West Palm Beach, Florida. His wife, Kathleen, whom he stabbed to death in their home at 906 Jewell Street (GPS: 30.25173 / -97.758896), was buried in Rosenberg, Texas. In his suicide note, Whitman claimed that he killed his mother and wife to spare them the humiliation he was about to bring on his family.

Several massacre artifacts—including Whitman's diary and personal effects, oral histories of several witnesses, and all the police records—are housed today in the Austin Public Library's History Center, 810 Guadalupe Street (GPS: 30.271667 / -97.745833). The public may view most of these items during normal business hours.

For two years after the mass murder, the tower's observation deck was closed. After it reopened in 1968, a series of suicide leaps forced it to close again in 1974. Finally, after several safety improvements, it reopened in 1999.

Today, tower tour guides are instructed not to talk about the Whitman massacre, but during the "self-guided" tour of the observation deck—which is usually shadowed by a campus policeman—you might get a few answers if you take your docent aside privately. Leave purses, backpacks, fanny packs, and other carrying bags in your car. Be prepared to go through a metal detector; the university remains skittish about evil-doers getting to the top of the tower with weapons.

In 2006—forty years after the massacre—the university mounted a bronze plaque beside a turtle pond just north of the tower (GPS: 30.28697 / -97.73953) as a memorial "to those who died, to those who were wounded, and to the countless other victims who were immeasurably affected by the tragedy." This is the only memorial to the tragedy on the UT campus.

In 2008 Travis County honored the police and citizen heroes of the massacre by naming a county facility in Oak Hill the Tower Heroes Building. It is at 8656-B West TX 71, about 12 miles from the tower.

The crime was explored in *A Sniper in the Tower* by Gary Lavergne (University of North Texas Press, 1997).

Also see "Victim Kathy Whitman's Grave" (Rosenberg).

TEXAS RANGERS HEADQUARTERS
Austin

The headquarters are in the Texas Department of Public Safety building, 5805 North Lamar Street. GPS: 30.326888 / -97.72451

The Texas Rangers are the most storied lawmen in the world. They've collected almost as many legends as criminals since they formed in 1835 to protect settlers in this Mexican territory from Indian raiders. In those early years it was said a Texas Ranger could "ride like a Mexican, trail like an Indian, shoot like a Tennessean, and fight like the devil." And in 1836, when Colonel William B. Travis begged for eleventh-hour help to defend the Alamo, the only men who came were Texas Rangers.

The Rangers dispersed during the Civil War but reconstituted in 1874. They quickly made their mark on Old West mythology by tracking down some of the frontier's baddest outlaws, like John Wesley Hardin and Sam Bass.

As the Old West gave way to a New West where bootlegging, boomtowns, and bank robberies were big business, the Rangers adapted. Aside from being America's original Border Patrol, they occasionally found themselves embroiled in international skirmishes, political corruption, and espionage cases.

In 1935—not long after Ranger Frank Hamer ended Bonnie and Clyde's crime spree—the Rangers officially became Texas's state bureau of investigation under the newly created Department of Public Safety, but even modern bureaucracy couldn't stifle the myth-making. The Texas Rangers' legend was so large and so wide that when U.S. Army Rangers landed in France during World War II, German newspapers mistakenly reported they were Texas Rangers, sending a collective shiver down the spines of German citizens.

In the modern era, the Rangers have solved murders, busted organized crime and illegal gambling operations, chased escaped German POWs during World War II, guarded campus integration during the civil rights era, thwarted drug and human smuggling, reopened cold cases, and conducted ultramodern forensic analysis.

The "lone" Ranger is no media contrivance. Throughout their fabled history, the Texas Rangers have been outnumbered, a proud fact. "One riot, one Ranger" is their unofficial motto. So maybe it won't surprise you to know that there are fewer than 140 sworn Texas Rangers.

RANGER FRANK HAMER'S GRAVE
Austin

Austin Memorial Park Cemetery is at 2800 Hancock Drive. The grave is in Block 1, Lot 48, only about 100 feet from the cemetery office. GPS: 30.32825 / -97.74986

The most renowned Texas Ranger of all, Frank Hamer (1884–1955), was one of four brothers who wore the Rangers' silver or gold star. When he became a Ranger in 1906, he rode horses, but when criminals got cars, so did Frank Hamer and the Rangers.

Hamer was fifty years old and had already retired from the Rangers when they rehired him in 1934 as a "special investigator" to track down Bonnie Parker and Clyde Barrow, two vicious young Texas bandits terrorizing the Midwest and South. Three months later, the star-crossed lovers were gunned down by Hamer and his posse on a rural road near Gibsland, Louisiana.

The 6-foot-3 Hamer retired again to become a strike-breaker for various oil companies but was recalled to the Rangers in 1948 to investigate a political corruption scandal involving senatorial candidate Lyndon B. Johnson.

In 1967, twelve years after his death at age seventy-one, Hamer's local legend blossomed worldwide when the hit film *Bonnie and Clyde* featured him (played by actor Denver Pyle, who's buried in an unmarked grave at Forreston, Texas, at GPS: 32.23009 / -96.86845) as a dyspeptic, shambling galoot. His wife and son sued the producers and reportedly won an out-of-court settlement.

Frank Hamer became the most famous Texas Ranger after bringing down Bonnie and Clyde.

More recently the 1998 film *The Newton Boys* suggested Hamer arrested Texas bank-robber Jess Newton in 1924. In reality, it was Frank Hamer's brother Harrison who busted Jess.

For book-lovers, author James Michener is buried nearby (GPS: 30.19949 / -97.45192).

Also see "Newton Gang's Graves" (Uvalde).

OAKWOOD CEMETERY
Austin

Oakwood Cemetery is at 1601 Navasota Street, or GPS 30.276292 / -97.728453.

This historic cemetery is literally full of stories from Texas's outlaw past. From lawmen to bad men to victims of one of America's earliest known serial killers, among the graves you'll find in this peaceful old boneyard are these:

- Gunfighter/lawman "Big Ben" Thompson (1843–1884) was a tough customer with one foot on each side of the law. Austin's city marshal was also quick to shoot anybody who displeased him, claiming to have killed thirty-two men. A gambler, drinker, and convicted murderer, he was a lethal friend to some of the Old West's most colorful figures, from Wyatt Earp to Wild Bill Hickok. In 1884 he was ambushed at San Antonio's Vaudeville Theater, where he had killed the popular owner Jack Harris two years before. Nobody was prosecuted, and his body was returned to Austin for burial here. (Block 1, Lot 71, or GPS 30.27583 / -97.72717)

- Officer Cornelius Fahey (1840–1875), an Irish-born cop, was shot by a late-night drunk and became the first Austin policeman ever killed in the line of duty. (Block 4, Lot 219, or GPS 30.27750 / -97.72681)

Ben Thompson was an Austin marshal, but he was also a notorious killer and gambler.

- Ranger Joe McKidrict (1861–1894) was murdered during a bordello brouhaha by an improbably named outlaw (and ex-Ranger) named Bass Outlaw in El Paso in 1894. His real name was Joe Coolly, and McKidrict was reportedly an alias he used to hide from his mother. Oddly, the headstone misses Joe's age and death date by a year. (His grave is in the Old Graveyard at GPS 30.27545 / -97.72827)

- Ranger John B. Armstrong (1850–1913) joined the Rangers about the time outlaw John Wesley Hardin escaped from custody and fled Texas. Although shot in the leg and walking with a cane, Armstrong asked for permission to hunt down Hardin. In 1877 Armstrong single-handedly confronted Hardin and four gang members on a Florida train. He killed one of the henchmen, coldcocked Hardin, and disarmed the other three. Hardin went to prison for seventeen years, and Armstrong became a cattle rancher—and in 2006 his family ranch was the site of a famous hunting accident involving Vice President Dick Cheney. The 2001 film *Texas Rangers* is built around Armstrong's exploits. He is a Texas Ranger Hall of Famer. (Block 2, Lot 777, or GPS 30.27612 / -97.72580)

- Irish saloonkeeper Mark Wilson (1844–1876) was just one of the thirty-two men gunslinger "Big Ben" Thompson claimed to have killed in his deadly career. Wilson was merely trying to keep Thompson from disrupting a show at his "variety theater" when a shootout erupted, and Wilson was shot four times. The killer and his victim now lie only about 120 yards from each other for eternity. (Block 2, Lot 403, or GPS 30.27552 / -97.72608)

- All eight victims of a serial killer who terrorized Austin in 1884 and 1885—three years before Britain's Jack the Ripper and ten years before America's "first" serial killer, H. H. Holmes—are buried in Oakwood. The first five victims of the killer, dubbed the "Servant Girl Annihilator" by local writer William Sidney Porter (aka O. Henry), were poor black women, mostly domestics, who were bludgeoned, stabbed, raped, and axe-murdered after being dragged from their beds into the night; a sixth person, the husband of one of the victims, was also killed during one of the attacks. Likely due to the low socioeconomic status of the victims, the case didn't rile the Austin public until Christmas Eve 1885, when two wealthy white socialites were axe-murdered. Then, as quickly as the year of terror had begun, it ended.

The case remains unsolved, though some amateur sleuths have surmised that the Servant Girl Annihilator might actually have abandoned Austin and moved to London, where he got a new nickname: Jack the Ripper. One modern FBI profiler's off-the-cuff analysis suggested that the killer was a black man who was abused as a child and who probably worked in a local butcher shop and had regular contact with his victims, perhaps delivering meats. Some eerie parallels also exist between the Servant Girl Annihilator case and the Axeman of New Orleans (1918–1919), another unsolved serial killing.

The Servant Girl Annihilator's first six victims—Mollie Smith, Eliza Shelley, Irene Cross, eleven-year-old Mary Ramey, Gracie Vance, and Orange Washington—were all buried in unmarked graves in Oakwood's "colored section," a sadly uncluttered acre just behind the cemetery office (GPS: 30.27690 / -97.72794).

Susan Hancock, one of two wealthy white women killed on Christmas Eve 1885, was dragged from her bed, raped in an alley, cleaved with an axe, and had an ice pick jabbed into her brain through her ear. Her husband, an unlikely suspect, was charged with the murder, but a hung jury freed him. She was buried in the cemetery's older section (Block 2, Lot 459, or GPS 30.27532 / -97.72528).

An hour after Hancock's slaying, the murder of white housewife Eula Phillips in the wealthiest section of Austin sent a new shudder through the capital's society. But here the case takes a strange twist: Eula's husband, Jimmy, also wounded in the attack, was charged with her murder. It seems Eula—or Luly, as she was known professionally—had been working as a prostitute behind her husband's back. Prosecutors say he killed her in a jealous rage, and the lurid trial shed light on the sexual peccadilloes of several of Austin's business and political leaders. Jimmy was convicted by a jury, but the verdict was later overturned on appeal. Eula's grave, in the oldest section of the cemetery where many stones are missing, weathered, or broken, has never been found.

TEXAS STATE LIBRARY AND ARCHIVES
Austin

The library and archives are at 1201 Brazos Street, just east of the capitol. No admission fee, but if you want to see certain documents, you will be asked for proper ID. GPS: 30.273995 / -97.738634

The newly renovated state archives is a treasure trove for historic crime researchers and curious buffs, ranging from original documents about outlaws Sam Bass and John Wesley Hardin to historic prison ledgers and a Clyde Barrow "wanted" poster. They don't advertise this, but if you ask kindly, they might let you see the business suit that Governor John Connally was wearing as he rode with President John F. Kennedy through Dealey Plaza on November 22, 1963. Controversially, it was dry-cleaned after the assassination.

The Murder of Madalyn Murray O'Hair

Once celebrated as "the most hated woman in America," atheist Madalyn Murray O'Hair (1919–1995) had plenty of reasons to fear for her safety. She had instigated the landmark Supreme Court ruling that ended prayer in public schools and unsuccessfully tried to defect to the Soviet Union during the Cold War. She was even a key aide in *Hustler* publisher Larry Flynt's 1980 presidential campaign.

O'Hair moved to Austin in 1963 and founded the American Atheists. On August 27, 1995, O'Hair, her son Jon Garth Murray, and granddaughter Robin disappeared from their home at 3702 Greystone Avenue (GPS: 30.359269 / -97.754518), leaving a terse note at their American Atheists headquarters (7215 Cameron Road, or GPS 30.327053 / -97.691315). A lot of money was missing, and many speculated the three had stolen it and fled.

Six years later, however, a federal investigation focused on David Roland Waters, an ex-con and former office manager of American Atheists who had embezzled $54,000 during O'Hair's tenure and who fantasized about murdering O'Hair in grisly ways. In a plea deal, Waters finally confessed. He had imprisoned the three for a month in a San Antonio apartment (Room 11 of the Warren Inn Village at 5050 Fredericksburg Road, or GPS 29.500605 / -98.558006), then killed them—plus a cohort.

Waters led cops to the shallow grave on a Hill Country ranch where he'd buried the rotting, mutilated remains (identifiable only through DNA, dental records, and O'Hair's prosthetic hip). He told investigators he'd extorted $500,000 in gold coins by kidnapping the O'Hairs. He and his girlfriend spent $80,000, but the rest (ironically) was stolen from a storage locker by burglars. Waters was convicted of extortion and money laundering—not kidnapping and murder—and imprisoned for life. He died in a North Carolina federal prison of lung cancer in 2003.

The O'Hairs' remains were given to Madalyn's only remaining son, William, a Baptist minister who buried or disposed of them secretly. Asked if prayers would be said at their graves, William replied: "They are already either in Heaven or Hell. Praying over them now will not make a difference."

TEXAS STATE CEMETERY
Austin

The Texas State Cemetery is at 909 Navasota Street. GPS: 30.267184 / -97.726669

Many of the most renowned figures in Texas history—including Stephen F. Austin, thirteen former governors, nine U.S. senators or representatives, fourteen signers of the Texas Declaration of Independence, and nineteen Texas Rangers—are buried here. Among the graves are the following:

- Ranger William "Bigfoot" Wallace (1817–1899) was an Indian fighter and revolutionary who reportedly descended from Scottish hero William Wallace. "Bigfoot" was one of the early Rangers and fought alongside heroes like Samuel Walker and Jack Hays on his way to becoming a Texas Ranger Hall of Famer. His grave is in the Republic Hill Section 2, Row K, Space 1 (GPS: 30.26532 / -97.72710).

- Ranger John R. Hughes (1855–1947) is said to be the inspiration for *The Lone Ranger*. The former cowboy and trapper joined the Rangers in 1887 after tracking several members of Butch Cassidy's Hole in the Wall Gang. Around 1900 a young writer named Zane Grey began riding with Hughes and in 1914 wrote a novel based on Hughes's exploits called *The Lone Ranger,* which he dedicated to his friend. Hughes, a lifelong bachelor who committed suicide at age ninety-two, is a Ranger Hall of Famer. (Republic Hill Section 2, Row S, Space 15, or GPS 30.26567 / -97.72719)

- Texas Supreme Court Justice William Pierson (1871–1935) and his wife, Lena, were shot to death on a road near Austin on April 24, 1935—just a week after he lamented the rise in violence and murder cases before the court. Their son, Howard Pierson, a twenty-year-old University of Texas student, claimed two robbers killed his parents, but he later confessed to the crime. He was judged insane and committed to an asylum, but in 1963 he was acquitted in a murder trial and set free to enjoy nearly a million dollars that had accumulated from his dead parents' estate. He later drowned. (Republic Hill Section 1, Row E, Space 22, or GPS 30.26521 / -97.72693)

- Confederate general, judge, and U.S. diplomat Alexander Terrell (1827–1912) is credited with writing a flattering poem about Lincoln assassin John Wilkes Booth, "Our

Brutus," that became a popular song in the postwar South. (Republic Hill Section 1, Row J, Space 26, or GPS 30.265367 / -97.7271)

- Governor John B. Connally (1917–1993) rode in the limo seat just in front of President Kennedy when he was assassinated in Dallas in 1963. Connally was also wounded in the attack, likely by a bullet that had already hit the president. (Republic Hill Section 2, Row P, Space 9, or GPS 30.26558 / -97.72720)

GRAVE OF OFFICER JOHN GAINES
Austin

Evergreen Cemetery is at 3304 East 12th Street. The grave is in Section A, Lot 410. GPS: 30.27751 / -97.69943

John Gaines (1863–1913) was Austin's only African-American cop at a time when blacks weren't allowed to arrest white criminals. One night Gaines came across a white constable disturbing the peace, so he called the police station for backup. While he was on the phone, the constable shot him to death.

O. HENRY MUSEUM AND HOUSE
Austin

The museum is at 409 East Fifth Street. Open Wednesday through Sunday from noon to 5:00 p.m. Free admission. GPS: 30.26566 / -97.73908

O. Henry was the pen name of short-story author William Sidney Porter (1862–1910), who lived in this Queen Anne cottage from 1893 to 1895. He is included here for two reasons: It was the creative Porter who named Austin's 1880s serial killer—who predated Britain's Jack the Ripper and America's H. H. Holmes—the "Servant

Girl Annihilator." He also is an outlaw himself, having had a habit of embezzling from the Texas banks where he worked. He served three years in federal prison, where he began writing stories under the pseudonym O. Henry.

Also see "Oakwood Cemetery" (Austin).

HORNSBY BEND CEMETERY
Austin

This private cemetery is on Hornsby Bend Cemetery Road, off FM 969 E (East MLK Boulevard), east of Austin. The road is sometimes closed to visitors. GPS: 30.256565 / -97.622033

Only two Texas cemeteries (Kerr County's Center Point and Austin's Texas State) boast more Texas Rangers than this one, but none can claim so many from one family. On a single-lane dirt road east of metropolitan Austin, this family cemetery contains twelve Texas Rangers from the Hornsby family dating back to the 1830s, plus three others. Another four commemorative markers memorialize four more Ranger relatives buried elsewhere. Oh, and in case you love baseball: Hall of Famer Rogers Hornsby (1896–1963), another famous relative, is buried here, too.

LYNDON BAINES JOHNSON PRESIDENTIAL LIBRARY
Austin

The library is at 2313 Red River Street, on the west side of I-35. Free admission. GPS: 30.285234 / -97.728109

In his 1,886 turbulent days as president, one still haunts the legacy of Lyndon Baines Johnson: November 22, 1963. Although LBJ's presidential library at the University of Texas highlights his leadership in the civil rights movement, the Great Society, Vietnam, and the War on Poverty, the assassination of John F. Kennedy lies like a dark shadow across the place.

The library holds extensive material related to the assassination, including documents, photos, tapes, oral histories, and some personal artifacts. In 2003 Nellie Connally—the former Texas first lady who rode with her husband in JFK's fateful limo that day— also donated her handwritten notes and the dress she was wearing the day of the assassination.

GUNSLINGER BILL THOMPSON'S GRAVE
Bastrop

Fairview Cemetery is on TX 95, about 1 mile north of the intersection with TX 71. The grave is in the extreme northwest corner of Block C. GPS: 30.11539 / -97.30485

The younger brother of legendary bad man Ben Thompson, gambler and gunslinger Billy Thompson (1846–1897) was still a daunting force. A Confederate veteran, vagabond, drunkard, shootist, and one-time owner of a Texas brothel with madam-wife Libby "Squirrel Tooth Alice" Thompson . . . well, his vices certainly added thrill to the British-born Billy's life.

Although well known as a killer, he eluded justice his entire life, often with the help of brother Ben. After Ben was assassinated in San Antonio's Vaudeville Theater in 1884, Texas braced for Billy's bloody vengeance against his brother's killers, but it never happened and Billy all but disappeared. When he died in 1897 of a stomach ailment at age fifty-one, the *San Antonio Express* eulogized him as being not "as hard a citizen" as Ben and praised his restraint for only putting six notches in his gun when he most certainly could have killed more.

His ex-wife, Libby, died in a Los Angeles rest home in 1953 at age ninety-eight.

Also see "Oakwood Cemetery" (Austin) and "Fatal Corner Crime Scene" (San Antonio).

GRAVE OF MADAM RITA AINSWORTH
Beaumont

Forest Lawn Memorial Park is at 4955 Pine Street. The grave is in Section C, Lot 9, Space 19. GPS: 30.12722 / -94.09860

Rita Ainsworth (1893–1978) is the best known of the many madams who worked Beaumont's rip-roaring bawdy houses, popular with oil roughnecks, seamen, and bankers alike. Her downtown Dixie Hotel—sometimes called "the most notorious bordello in the South"—was shuttered in 1961 by crusading legislators, although the turn-of-the-century building still exists on the renovated Crockett Street as a nightclub. A nearby restaurant, Rio Rita's, preserves her name in every menu with a romantic (and fictional) story. Her slightly racy epitaph reads, "For the love you gave your fellow man—eternal roses."

VIGILANTE SCOTT COOLEY'S GRAVE
Blanco

To reach Miller Creek Cemetery, drive about 5.3 miles north of Blanco on US 281, then go east (right) on US 290 for about 2.1 miles. GPS: 30.196267 / -98.33215

Scott Cooley (1852–1876) isn't well known, but his story is made for Hollywood. An orphan who was adopted by a local rancher named Tim Williamson, he grew up to be a Texas Ranger. But when his adoptive father was murdered by a lynch mob in a central Texas range feud called the "Hoodoo War," Cooley quit the Rangers and turned into a vicious vigilante. He relentlessly hunted the dozen or so killers one by one. Among his cohorts was Johnny Ringo, who gained infamy later for his personal war with the Earps in Tombstone. Cooley himself eluded justice but died at age twenty-four of "brain fever"—though many believe he was poisoned.

Also see "Deputy John Whorlie (or Worley) Death Site" (Mason).

LYNCHED HORSE-THIEVES' COMMON GRAVE
Blue

Burns Cemetery lies just north of Blue, a rural community about 9 miles west of Lexington on FM 696. You'll see a sign pointing the way to the cemetery, which lies less than a mile north of FM 696. GPS: 30.39370 / -97.15195

Gun-wielding, masked vigilantes interrupted a country dance in June 1877 and called out the names of young men they accused of being horse thieves. Four of the men—brothers-in-law John Kuykendall, Wade Alsup, Young Floyd, and Blake Scott—were taken from the dance and hanged from the limb of a tree (now cut down) about 100 yards away. (A fifth suspect escaped the hanging because he was in the outhouse when his buddies were nabbed.) The next morning, friends went out to retrieve the bodies and found that their weight had bent the tree limb and their feet were touching the ground.

All four are buried together here; only the Kuykendall family could afford a headstone. Very near—possibly one of the adjacent small metal crosses—is the unmarked grave of Wade Alsup's father, Horace, who was also assassinated by a vigilante two years later.

WILD BILL HICKOK'S LAST VICTIM
Brenham

Prairie Lea Cemetery is at the intersection of Prairie Lea and West Fifth Streets. GPS: 30.15606 / -96.40901

Gambler and gunman Philip Houston Coe (1839–1871) hung out with a tough crowd. His best buddy was gunslinger "Big Ben" Thompson, he gambled with John Wesley Hardin, and he courted trouble with Abilene (Kansas) marshal James Butler "Wild Bill" Hickok. Bad blood rose when saloon-keeper Coe and Hickok both fancied the same lovely hooker. On October 5, 1871, Hickok killed Coe (and his own deputy) in a wild shootout in the streets of Abilene.

He was Hickok's last known victim before Wild Bill himself was murdered in Deadwood, South Dakota, in 1876.

LONGHORN CAVERNS
Burnet

The caverns are about 6 miles west and 6 miles south of Burnet on Park Road 4, off US 281. GPS: 30.684722 / -98.350833

This 645-acre state park contains one of the world's most unique caves, carved by water in limestone over thousands of years. More recently, the extensive caverns made a perfect outlaw hideout. Some legends say the train-robbing Sam Bass hid $2 million in loot here, although it's never been found. Other bandits hid out in the caves occasionally, too. During the Civil War, rebels reportedly made gunpowder in the caverns' relatively cool and safe recesses. Texas Rangers rescued a little girl here kidnapped by Indians. And during Prohibition, a nightclub actually operated inside. Today, guided tours are available.

RANGER LEANDER McNELLY'S GRAVE
Burton

Mount Zion Cemetery is on the east side of FM 1948 (near the intersection with FM 390), about a mile northeast of Burton. GPS: 30.21401 / -96.57642

Although he was only 5-foot-6 and 130 pounds, and suffered from tuberculosis most of his short life, Leander McNelly (1844–1877) looms as one of the biggest Texas Rangers.

At age seventeen he enlisted in the Confederate Army as a private; by nineteen, he was a captain. McNelly was celebrated for his guerrilla tactics, which often overcame greater forces. After the war, he joined the Texas State Police and then the Texas Rangers.

Ranger Leander McNelly led a vicious "special mission" to clean up Texas's dangerous Nueces Strip.

In 1875 McNelly was appointed to command a "special force" of Rangers to clean up the lawless area between the Nueces River and the Rio Grande known as the Nueces Strip, where brigands like King Fisher and Juan Cortina marauded freely. But his tactics were as controversial as they were punitive. His men often crossed illegally into Mexico chasing rustlers and bandits, at least once touching off an international incident, and his prisoners were tortured and hanged without trial. In 1875, after one of McNelly's Rangers was murdered, he killed twelve rustlers and stacked their corpses "like cordwood" in Brownsville's Market Square (GPS: 25.902517 / -97.497267).

Credited with taming the Nueces Strip, McNelly retired to his Burton farm in 1876, where he died in 1877 from tuberculosis. He was only thirty-three. Grateful citizens of South Texas collected money to erect a towering monument over his grave.

McNelly was portrayed by actor Dylan McDermott in the 2001 Hollywood western *Texas Rangers,* which was very loosely based on the 1962 memoir *Taming the Nueces Strip* by one of McNelly's Rangers, George Durham. McNelly is in the Texas Ranger Hall of Fame.

Also see "Outlaw King Fisher's Grave" (Uvalde).

Remembering Selena

Grammy-winning Tejano singing star Selena Quintanilla-Perez (1971–1995) was poised to be a star of mainstream pop music when she was gunned down in Corpus Christi by a disgruntled employee in March 1995. She was only twenty-three. Like so many other prematurely dead stars, she became an almost mythic figure, especially among young Latinos. But ironically, her murder also introduced her to a much bigger audience.

Selena began singing at age ten with her father's band, and at sixteen she was the Tejano Music Association's female vocalist of the year. She released her first album in 1990 and won a 1994 Grammy for her album *Live.* She also appeared in the Johnny Depp movie *Don Juan DeMarco,* which was released after her death along with an English-singing album that was to appeal to non-Latino audiences.

25

Trouble began when Selena suspected Yolanda Saldivar, her fan club president and manager of her chain of salons and boutiques, of embezzling $30,000. When she confronted Saldivar in a Corpus Christi motel room, Saldivar pulled a .38-caliber handgun from her purse and shot Selena once in the back. Screaming profanities, Saldivar chased Selena to the hotel lobby, where she collapsed. She died at the hospital shortly after.

Saldivar, who held police at bay for almost ten hours after the shooting, was convicted of first-degree murder and sentenced to life in prison. She becomes eligible for parole the day before the thirtieth anniversary of Selena's murder in 2025.

Two years after the slaying, Hollywood told the story in *Selena,* starring Jennifer Lopez in her breakthrough film role. Today several sites mark Selena's life and death, all visited by thousands every year.

The shooting happened in Room 158 at the Days Inn at 901 Navigation Boulevard (GPS: 27.80226 / -97.45353), but don't bother hunting for the room. After the murder the hotel's management renumbered all the rooms to forestall a tidal wave of bereaved fans.

Selena's lavish grave is at Seaside Memorial Park, 4357 Ocean Drive (GPS: 27.73239 / -97.36244). It is enclosed in a black iron railing and features a large bronze sculpture of the young singer, who lies beneath a small oak.

A shrinelike memorial, *Mirador del Flor* (Overlook of the Flower), was erected in Selena's honor on Corpus Christi's seawall at Peoples Street (GPS: 27.79667 / -97.39108). The spot has become a "quasi-holy ground," according to a local professor of Mexican-American studies. Here a life-size statue of Selena looks out to sea, and so might you: After her trial, Saldivar's gun was destroyed and its pieces scattered in Corpus Christi Bay.

Selena's family has turned part of her recording studio into a museum, too. A public area exists in Q Productions' building at 5410 Leopard Street (GPS: 27.79757 / -97.46141) and contains personal memorabilia, several stage outfits, and Selena's red Porsche. And although it's not related to Selena's murder, her childhood home still exists. It's at 709 Bloomington Street (GPS: 27.75695 / -97.450385).

Fans flock daily to Selena's grave in Seaside Memorial Park.

SERIAL KILLER JOE BALL'S GRAVE AND TAVERN
Elmendorf

The grave is in St. Anthony of Padua Catholic Cemetery, about 1.3 miles southwest from US 181 on Kilowatt Road. GPS: 29.259117 / -98.329883

Not yet known as the infamous "Butcher of Elmendorf," young Joe Ball (1896–1938) returned from World War I to become a bootlegger. After Prohibition he opened a roadhouse near his hometown of Elmendorf and called it the Sociable Inn, where he hired pretty waitresses and kept a pond full of live alligators out back. For his customers' enjoyment, the sadistic Ball would often feed live dogs and cats to his gators.

So when his waitresses started disappearing, the locals joked he must have fed them to the gators, too. The jokes stopped when a neighbor claimed to have seen Ball carving meat off a human body and tossing it to his alligators. Deputies John Gray and Johnny Klevenhagen went to the Sociable Inn to interview him, but before they could ask a single question, Ball shot himself in the heart with a .45-caliber revolver. In the days to come, Ball's handyman showed cops where he had helped to bury the corpses of two victims, Minnie Gotthardt and Hazel Brown—a crime for which he spent two years in prison.

Joe Ball's Sociable Inn (7843 FM 327 in Elmendorf, or GPS 29.253983 / -98.336683) still exists today, though it is a private home now (*don't trespass*). And the pit out back where Ball kept his hungry pet alligators—which might have helped him dispose of some victims—is still there, too, hidden by a shed built above it. This is where Ball killed himself rather than be interrogated by suspicious detectives.

Are there other long-missing victims who died here and whose remains were digested by Ball's beloved gators? We'll likely never know exactly how many people Joe Ball murdered, but we know his allegedly man-eating pets were donated to the San Antonio Zoo, where they lived out their years as kiddie curiosities.

Ball's story inspired Tobe Hooper's 1977 horror flick, *Eaten Alive,* in which a deranged hotel owner butchers his guests and feeds them to his pet alligator out back.

Also see "Victim Minnie Gotthardt's Grave" (Aransas Pass), "Victim Hazel Brown's Grave" (Knobbs Springs), and "Ranger Johnny Klevenhagen's Grave" (San Antonio).

BABY GRACE MEMORIAL
Galveston

Riley's Island is an uninhabited barrier island in Galveston Bay, just south of Karankawa Lake, reachable only by boat. GPS: 29.236876 / -95.01792

In the summer of 2007, a fisherman made a grisly discovery: the rotten corpse of a child in a plastic storage bin on a distant barrier island in Galveston Bay. For months in the national media, the little girl was known only as Baby Grace.

But when an Ohio woman recognized the reconstructed face as her two-year-old granddaughter, Riley Ann Sawyers, the investigation took a new turn. Police arrested the toddler's mother, Kim Trenor, and stepfather, Royce Zeigler, a Spring couple who admitted the child was killed during a torturous "discipline" session in which she was smothered with pillows, beaten with a belt, held under cold water, and thrown against a wall. Her body was hidden in a storage shed for several weeks until it was set adrift in the plastic bin, which washed ashore on the small island.

Local police and citizens erected a modest memorial to Baby Grace/Riley Ann Sawyers on the spot where she was found, but it was washed away by Hurricane Ike in 2008. The island has since been renamed Riley's Island. Riley's remains were eventually buried near her birthplace in Ohio.

BALINESE ROOM SITE
Galveston

The site is at 2107 Seawall, on the beach at the end of 21st Street. GPS: 29.290278 / -94.785833

Galveston was once among America's roughest cities—and one of the landmarks of the island's criminal past was the Balinese Room. In 1923 bootlegging brothers Sam and Rosario Maceo's Sui Jen Chinese restaurant offered egg noodles, whiskey, and illicit

THE CRIME BUFF'S GUIDE TO OUTLAW TEXAS

gambling on a 200-foot pier over Galveston Bay. During Prohibition it was a speakeasy and casino. In the midst of World War II, they expanded and gave the place a more tropical name: the Balinese Room.

In the nightclub's heyday, the Maceos brought in some of the biggest names in showbiz, including Jack Benny, George Burns and Gracie Allen, Duke Ellington, Bob Hope, Groucho Marx, and Frank Sinatra. When Texas Rangers raided the popular nightspot occasionally, the house band would strike up a rousing rendition of "The Eyes of Texas Are Upon You" as the Rangers came through the club's famous red door, a signal to back-room casino workers that the cops were coming. By the time the Rangers got to the gaming room, all evidence was hidden.

Legend has it that a Balinese bartender mixed up a new drink for singer Peggy (Margaret) Lee in 1948 and named it after her, in Spanish: the margarita. In 1957 the nightclub closed, and the Balinese Room became a tourist trap. But what the Texas Rangers couldn't do completely, Mother Nature did: 2008's Hurricane Ike stripped the entire historic structure down to the old pilings.

BOXER JACK JOHNSON'S ARREST
Galveston

Harmony Hall once stood on the site now occupied by the historic Harmony Masonic Lodge, 2128 Church Street. GPS: 29.304157 / -94.79196

The childhood home of Galveston native Jack Johnson (1878–1946) at 808 Broadway (GPS: 29.304691 / -94.775279) was destroyed in the calamitous 1900 hurricane, but the young dockworker stayed on the island to make money in illegal boxing matches. In 1901 at Harmony Hall (now the Harmony Masonic Lodge), veteran boxer Joe Choynski KO'd young Johnson in an outlaw bout—and the two were quickly arrested by Texas Rangers. In jail, Choynski tutored the young Johnson. A grand jury failed to indict the two fighters but urged them to get out of town, thus beginning a boxing career that would make Jack Johnson, the son of former slaves, the heavy-weight champion of the world—and one of America's most contro-versial athletes long before Cassius Clay was born.

In 1913 the brash Johnson was convicted for having a relation-ship with a white woman, but he jumped bail and lived abroad as a fugitive. He surrendered in 1920 and spent a year in Leavenworth (where he invented a special wrench that was patented in 1922). Efforts have been made in Congress to secure a full presidential pardon for Johnson.

Johnson's story has been told in many forms, including the 2005 Ken Burns documentary *Unforgivable Blackness* and Dr. Al-Tony Gilmore's 1975 biography *Bad Nigger!* A 1967 play and 1970 movie, *The Great White Hope*, were loosely based on Johnson's life.

PIRATE JEAN LAFITTE'S HOME
Galveston

The home site is at 1417 Avenue A, between present-day 14th and 15th Streets, near the Galveston wharf. GPS: 29.31045 / -94.78505

After being evicted from New Orleans in 1817, Jean Lafitte (ca. 1776–1823) and his fellow pirates established a colony on present-day Galveston Island, which they called Campeche. They built bungalows, pool halls, a shipyard, a slave market, saloons, and gambling halls—and a luxurious home for Lafitte. The two-story "Maison Rouge" (Red House) was furnished with pirate booty, sur-rounded by a moat, and painted red, and it was Lafitte's headquar-ters until these real-life pirates of the Caribbean were ousted by the U.S. Navy in 1821.

All the buildings, including Maison Rouge, were burned by the retreating buccaneers. Today only the original foundation and cellars of Maison Rouge exist beneath the ruins of another structure built in 1870.

Ah, but legends remain. While on Galveston Island, Lafitte married Madeline Rigaud, a French settler's widow. When she died during childbirth in 1820, Lafitte reportedly buried her beneath Maison Rouge with a large cache of gold. To this day, high-tech treasure-seekers still explore the site—with no luck.

RANGER JOHN TRUEHEART'S GRAVE
Galveston
Evergreen Cemetery is between 40th and 43rd Streets at Avenue K. GPS: 29.29355 / -94.81455

Among the first Texas Rangers hired, in 1841, John Trueheart (1801–1874) was rewarded for his service with a land grant outside Fort Davis. His family home still exists there as a bed-and-breakfast. A Texas historical marker tells his story in Evergreen's old section.

KILLER "WILD BILL" LONGLEY'S GRAVE
Giddings
Giddings City Cemetery is on the western edge of town, just south of US 290. GPS: 30.18315 / -96.94778

One of the Wild West's most prolific killers, William Longley (1851–1878) killed at least thirty-two men, and one woman, in his short life. But he was also one of the Wild West's luckiest outlaws, since almost no other could claim to have literally survived the hangman's noose twice.

Shortly after the fifteen-year-old Longley killed a black deputy for insulting his father, vigilantes caught him and lynched him. But as the posse was riding away, one of the vigilantes turned and fired two shots at the hanging killer. One bullet hit Longley's face and the other clipped the rope, inadvertently freeing Longley for another dozen years of murder and marauding throughout the West.

In 1878 Longley was sentenced to die for the murder of a Giddings man. Legend says he paused on the gallows' rickety stairs and joked that he didn't want to fall and break his neck. Clutching a religious medal and a celluloid flower, Longley confessed a few other crimes to hundreds of onlookers, then dropped through the hangman's trapdoor . . . but the rope was too long and Longley too tall, and he simply landed with both feet on the ground. So lucky Longley was hoisted back onto the scaffold and rehanged. The third time was a charm.

Ah, but that's where Longley's legend really gets interesting. His body, hated in death as much as in life, was buried in an unmarked grave outside the Giddings cemetery. A chunk of petrified wood was placed at the approximate spot almost fifty years later, but caretakers say the stone—not the body—was moved occasionally. So in 1986 Longley's descendants sought the help of one of America's top forensic anthropologists, Dr. Doug Owsley, to find their famous black sheep's grave. Over the next few years, Owsley's team dug up about thirty old graves in the Giddings cemetery but didn't find Longley. In 1998, using old photos and computer technology to identify land contours, the team found an unmarked grave that contained remains matching Longley's physical description, but more importantly, also contained a little religious medal and a celluloid flower. DNA from the corpse's tooth later matched a blood sample taken from a descendant of Longley's sister.

Today the cemetery has expanded to encompass Longley's grave. A stub of the old petrified-wood marker remains, along with a nondescript, broken slab and a state historical marker. And Longley himself has been renovated: He was romanticized by Rory Calhoun in the CBS TV series *The Texan* (1958–1960).

HANGING TREE
Goliad

The tree is on the north lawn of the Goliad County Courthouse in the town square, which is in the center of town three blocks south of US 59. GPS: 28.66620 / -97.39194

We'll go out on a limb here and say that hundreds of Old West trees were used to string up unlucky men and women, but very few still exist more than a hundred years later . . . and even fewer are official historical sites. But this magnificent live oak on the Goliad County Courthouse's front lawn is an authentic hanging tree, complete with several sturdy, low-hanging (no pun intended) branches. From 1846 to 1870 Goliad's condemned outlaws were often taken a few steps from the courthouse to this tree to be publicly executed. Nobody kept track of the dead, but some have estimated their number into the low hundreds.

Justice was as close as this old live oak for rustlers and killers convicted at Goliad's old courthouse.

GANGSTA RAPPER PIMP C'S GRAVE
Groves

Greenlawn Memorial Park is at 3900 Twin City Highway, between Groves and Port Arthur. Butler is in the Redeemer mausoleum in the outdoor Crypt 383, Row C. GPS: 29.935843 / -93.924211

Born in tough-fisted Port Arthur—just like Janis Joplin—Chad Butler (1973–2007) took the name Pimp C and teamed with friend Bun B as the Underground Kingz (UGK), whose profane, violent, and drug-infused rap had a dirty Dixie twang. But Pimp C wasn't just an urban poseur: In 2002 he was imprisoned for four years after brandishing a gun during an argument with a woman at a mall. His incarceration only enhanced his gangsta status, and when he got out in 2006, UGK recorded their Grammy-nominated eponymous album, *UGK*.

But Pimp C never enjoyed the album's success. Just four months after it debuted, he was found dead in his bed at the Mondrian Hotel in West Hollywood, California. He had died from an accidental overdose of "sizzurp"—an illegal cocktail of prescription cough syrup and fruit-flavored soda—which proved deadly when combined with his sleep apnea. And just like his homegirl Janis Joplin, Pimp C OD'd in a Los Angeles hotel room.

KILLER-WIDOW MARIE DACH'S GRAVE
High Hill

The Nativity of the Blessed Virgin Mary Cemetery is behind St. Mary Roman Catholic Church at 3833 FM 2672. The grave is in the older back portion of the graveyard, on the right side. GPS: 29.71721 / -96.92501

Shortly after her husband died of cancer, Marie Dach (1890–1933) hired fifty-five-year-old Henry Stoever to help on her 160-acre farm about 5 miles northwest of Schulenberg. Three years later, however, Henry went missing and his brother called the cops. Deputy Sheriff

T. J. Flournoy—yes, the same lawman who'd be at the center of the "best little whorehouse" storm forty years later—grew suspicious over a new henhouse on Dach's property. When he dug it up, he found Stoever's shot and charred corpse buried 7 feet down.

At her trial, Dach claimed she shot Stoever in his sleep after he attacked her, but Flournoy found $550 of Stoever's money in her possession. Although more than a hundred potential jurors refused to consider executing a woman, Dach was convicted and sentenced to die in the electric chair. She would have been the first Texas woman to be legally executed, but she died on a hunger strike in the Fayette County Jail three months after her death sentence was handed down, even before it was appealed. Some say her ghost still haunts the old jail.

What was left of Henry Stoever (1875–1933) was buried in the Freiburg Lutheran Cemetery on Salem-Freyburg Road off FM 2238, immediately south of the Salem Lutheran Cemetery (GPS: 29.73602 / -97.00715).

Also see "Best Little Whorehouse in Texas" (La Grange).

DOUBLE BANK ROBBERY
Hondo
Hondo is 43 miles west of San Antonio on US 90.

In one of the most audacious heists in American outlaw history, a gang of brothers known as the Newton Boys robbed not one, but two banks in this small town on the same January night in 1921. Luckily for the robbers, the first bank's night watchman was sleeping in the local railroad depot, so after cutting the town's phone lines, they quickly cracked the safe of the First National Bank at 1112 18th Street (GPS: 29.348296 / -99.141097) with nitroglycerine. In fact, the whole robbery was so efficient, the boys decided to go down the street and rob the Hondo State Bank at 1711 Avenue M (GPS: 29.348829 / -99.141687).

One of two banks robbed in the same night by the Newton Boys

The Newtons got away with nearly $5,000 in cash (mostly in silver coins) and another $25,000 to $30,000 in government bonds and war stamps. Although they spent more than two hours battering safe-deposit boxes with sledgehammers and blowing open both banks' safes with explosives, nobody ever heard a thing.

At the First National Bank (Hondo National Bank today), the Newtons simply forced open the front door. But if you go into the alley south of the old Hondo State Bank (vacant as of this writing) today, you'll see where tall, arched windows have been bricked up. The Newtons entered this bank by prying back the iron bars at the top of one of these windows.

The double robbery is depicted in the 1998 film *The Newton Boys,* starring Matthew McConaughey.

Also see "Newton Gang's Graves" (Uvalde).

FORMER ENRON HEADQUARTERS
Houston
The former headquarters are at 1400 Smith Street in downtown Houston. GPS: 29.7558 / -95.3713

This fifty-story, 1.27-million-square-foot tower was the mother ship of the scandalous energy company Enron, which screwed thousands of workers and investors out of tens of billions of dollars. As a result of the company's collapse, Enron's two top executives, Ken Lay and Jeff Skilling, faced myriad criminal charges. Skilling was sentenced to twenty-four years in federal prison, but Lay escaped justice by dying of a heart attack during an Aspen vacation before his sentencing. As a result, his conviction was vacated by the presiding judge as if it never happened.

Not convinced this is a Texas "outlaw" site? Consider this: The thieves who ran Enron stole more money than any hundred bank, train, or casino robbers you can name—all put together.

If you're looking for that big, cockeyed "E" logo, don't bother. That iconic symbol of American greed was removed in 2007 and auctioned off for a mere $44,000.

MURDER BY MERCEDES
Houston
Nassau Bay Hilton is at 3000 NASA Road One. The parking-lot crime scene is at (GPS: 29.555545 / -95.075389)

Houston orthodontist Dr. David Harris (1957–2002) and his dentist-wife, Clara, opened a successful chain of dental clinics after they were married on Valentine's Day in 1992. But ten years later, Clara suspected her husband was cheating on her with his lithe, sexy receptionist, and she hired a private investigator to find out.

On July 24, 2002, the private eye followed David and his mistress to a suburban hotel and called Clara, who rushed to the hotel in her $70,000 Mercedes with David's sixteen-year-old daughter to catch him red-handed. And she did.

After a scuffle in the hotel's parking lot, an enraged Clara got in her Mercedes and deliberately ran down David—then circled around the lot to hit her philandering husband at least twice more while David's screaming daughter watched. Surprisingly, the whole attack in the Nassau Bay Hilton's parking lot was videotaped by Clara's private investigator. David died at the scene.

David was buried in Pearland's South Park Cemetery (GPS: 29.58814 / -95.28986). Clara was convicted of murder in 2003 and sentenced to twenty years in prison and a $10,000 fine. She's eligible for parole in 2013. Ironically, David's marker bears Clara's name, as if she will be buried there, too.

The 2004 book *Out of Control* explored the killing.

MURDER OF WILLIAM MARSH RICE
Houston
William Marsh Rice's ashes are entombed under his statue in the Rice University Quadrangle. GPS: 29.718547 / -95.399051

A visionary entrepreneur, William Marsh Rice (1816–1900) was one of Houston's earliest movers and shakers—and one of its richest. He also dreamed of creating a college with profits he made from oil, retailing, and real estate. But some of his inner circle had different ideas for his money.

After Rice's second wife died in 1896, a dispute arose over her multimillion-dollar estate, imperiling his wish to build a university. Albert Patrick, a shady lawyer for the dead wife's estate, realized the untold riches at stake, so he conspired with Rice's personal valet, Charlie Jones, to kill Rice and steal as much of his money as they could.

On September 23, 1900, in Rice's New York apartment, Jones covered Rice's face with chloroform-soaked towels and the old man

The remains of murdered philanthropist William Marsh Rice were entombed in the base of his statue at Rice University.

died. Nobody suspected foul play until Patrick tried to cash forged checks at Rice's bank. Both men were arrested; Jones confessed and testified against Patrick, who was sentenced to die but was pardoned by the governor of New York after only ten years in prison.

Rice was cremated and his ashes sealed beneath a heroic statue of him on the campus of Houston's Rice University—established in 1904 with a $4.6 million endowment from his estate.

FOREST PARK–WESTHEIMER CEMETERY
Houston

The cemetery is at 12800 Westheimer Road, at the northwest corner of the intersection of Westheimer and Dairy Ashford Roads. GPS: 29.739444 / -95.608611

- Criminal lawyer Percy Foreman (1902–1988), the son of a small-town Texas sheriff, once tried to be a professional wrestler. But in more than sixty years as a criminal lawyer, Foreman lost only 53 of more than 1,500 murder cases—and only one client was actually executed. Known for his big fees, bigger theatrics, and biggest frame (6-foot-4 and 250 pounds), Foreman represented clients such as Martin Luther King assassin James Earl Ray and hit man Charles Harrelson, actor Woody's dad. (GPS: 29.73762 / -95.61082)

- The strangled corpse of would-be model Elena Semander (1962–1982) was found in a Houston dumpster in 1982. Police later discovered she was the fifth victim of serial killer Coral Watts, who was suspected in the murders of a hundred women, mostly in Texas and Michigan. Although he might be the most prolific serial killer in American history, Watts eluded prosecution for his thirteen Texas murders through a plea bargain. He was serving two life sentences in Michigan when he died of prostate cancer in 2007. (GPS: 29.74162 / -95.61028)

- Socialite murder-victim Joan Robinson Hill (1931–1969) is also buried here (GPS: 29.73855 / -95.60710). See Dr. John Hill under "Memorial Oaks Cemetery" (Houston).

FOREST PARK–LAWNDALE CEMETERY
(AKA GARDEN OF GETHSEMANE)
Houston
The cemetery is at 6900 Lawndale Street, between Griggs Road and South Wayside Drive. GPS: 29.721667 / -95.304167

- Texas hadn't executed a woman in 135 years when murderer Karla Faye Tucker's execution drew near, but she wasn't going quietly. Although Tucker (1959–1998) savagely killed her ex-lover and his new girlfriend, she found Jesus in jail and sought clemency as a born-again Christian who had learned the error of her ways. She even married her prison chaplain. Many Americans rallied around the pretty young woman on TV who didn't seem capable of whacking her ex-beau more than twenty times with a pickaxe. But the State of Texas and the U.S. Supreme Court weren't as forgiving, and Tucker became the first American woman executed in fourteen years. Her grave (GPS: 29.71775 / -95.30557) is in the southernmost one-third of the Acacia section, but don't bother asking cemetery staffers for her specific plot information . . . they won't tell you.

- Debra Sue Schatz (1960–1984) was the first female letter carrier killed in the line of duty. She was shot twice in the head by David Port, a seventeen-year-old boy who lived on her route. Port was sentenced to seventy-five years in prison but is expected to be released in 2011 after only twenty-six years. (GPS: 29.71314 / -95.30244)

- Timothy O'Bryan (1966–1974) was poisoned by his own father in a bizarre insurance scam on Halloween 1974. Dad Ronald O'Bryan spiked his children's Pixy Stix candies with cyanide to claim a $20,000 life-insurance policy. Only eight-year-old Timmy ate the candy, and his death set off a rash of Halloween safety programs nationwide. His father—who became famous as Houston's "Candyman" killer—was executed in 1984 and is buried 20 miles away; see his listing under "Forest Park East Cemetery" (Webster). Timothy's grave is at GPS 29.71296 / -95.30671.

- Ex-marine Donald Chambers (1930–1999) founded the out-law motorcycle gang known as the Bandidos in 1966. The name was inspired by a visit to a now-defunct museum in San Leon, Texas, and Chambers's own home at 702 North Eastwood Street (GPS: 29.754599 / -95.324984) was the first gang clubhouse. Under Chambers's leadership, the Bandidos became a serious rival to the more established Hell's Angels; today the Bandidos claim more than 2,400 members in sixteen countries. In 1972 Chambers and two other

Don Chambers founded the Bandidos motorcycle gang in 1966.

43

Bandidos murdered two El Paso drug dealers over a sour deal. Police say Chambers forced his victims to dig their own graves before shooting them and incinerating their corpses. Chambers was sentenced to a life term but served only about ten years. He died of colon cancer in 1999, and hundreds of Bandidos attended his burial here (GPS: 29.71766 / -95.30200). In June 2009 his daughter laid out an elaborate black memorial to satisfy his dying wish.

MEMORIAL OAKS CEMETERY
Houston

Memorial Oaks is at 15000 Memorial Drive, just south of I-10 between Dairy Ashford Road and North Eldridge Parkway. GPS: 29.78190 / -95.61500

- Born poor but devoutly religious in Waco, Leon Jaworski (1905–1982) was the youngest lawyer ever admitted to the Texas bar in 1925. He prosecuted war crimes committed at the Nazis' Dachau concentration camp and worked with the Warren Commission investigating the JFK assassination. But he is best known as the special prosecutor who investigated President Nixon's role in the Watergate break-in, and his work led directly to the release of incriminating White House tapes and Nixon's resignation in 1974. Jaworski died at age seventy-seven of a heart attack at his ranch near Wimberley while chopping wood, one of his favorite hobbies. His grave is at GPS 29.78234 / -95.61504.

- Did plastic surgeon Dr. John Hill (1931–1972) murder his rich, socialite wife Joan Robinson Hill in 1969 by poisoning her pastries and withholding necessary medical care?

Before that question could be answered in court, Dr. Hill was shot to death in his home by an ex-con hit man who was killed by cops before his trial. Two women, Lilla Paulus and Marcia McKittrick, were convicted of arranging the doctor's murder at the request of Joan Hill's millionaire oilman father, Ash Robinson, who was never charged. Dr. Hill's grave is here at GPS 29.78126 / -95.61564. Joan Hill was buried in Houston's Forest Park–Westheimer Cemetery. This strange case inspired two books, *Blood and Money* by Tommy Thompson and *Prescription Murder* by Ann Kurth, and the 1981 movie *Murder in Texas*, starring Katharine Ross and Sam Elliott.

WOODLAWN CEMETERY
Houston
The cemetery is at 1101 Antoine Drive, just north of I-10 at exit 762 west of Houston's downtown area. GPS: 29.78800 / -95.47620

- In one of the stranger tales of victimology, brothers Billy and Michael Baulch were both killed by the same Houston serial killer—one year apart. Billy, age seventeen, was abducted and murdered by sadistic pedophile Dean Corll in 1972. His body was buried on a High Island beach. A year later, his younger brother Michael, age sixteen, was also raped, tortured, and murdered before his corpse was buried in Corll's rented boat shed with sixteen other dead boys. The brothers are buried in the same unmarked grave in the Garden of Memories (GPS: 29.78960 / -95.47812). At least three more of Corll's twenty-seven known victims are buried in Woodlawn: Homer Garcia, Gregory Malley Winkle, and James Glass.

- Flamboyant TV reporter Marvin Zindler (1921–2007), whose stories led to the closing of the famed Chicken Ranch brothel in 1973, is buried in Beth Israel Memorial Gardens (GPS: 29.78918 / -95.47626), a small Jewish cemetery adjacent to Woodlawn. See more under "Best Little Whorehouse in Texas" (La Grange).

EXECUTED KILLER FRANCES NEWTON'S GRAVE
Houston

Paradise North Cemetery is at 10401 West Montgomery Road, northwest of the city center. Newton's grave is in the Garden of Memories, Plot 891N, Space 4. GPS: 29.885267 / -95.461283

Triple murderer Frances Newton (1965–2005) killed her exhusband and two daughters with a borrowed pistol. In 2005 she became the first black woman to be executed in the state of Texas since a slave girl was hanged in 1858.

CAPTAIN JOE BYRD CEMETERY
(AKA PECKERWOOD HILL)
Huntsville

The cemetery is 1 mile southeast of the Texas Penitentiary's Walls Unit on Bowers Boulevard, covering 22 acres between Sycamore and 16th Streets. GPS: 30.711 / -95.5363

The history of the American death penalty is scrawled across the handmade concrete headstones on Peckerwood Hill, Texas's biggest and oldest prison cemetery. More condemned men (180) are buried here than twenty-nine other states have executed in their entire history—altogether. Most share the ignominy of a nameless tombstone marked only with their inmate number, a death date, and a simple X . . . executed.

The more than 3,000 dead criminals on Peckerwood Hill are past caring. This place smells and feels different from other grave-yards. It's dark and sour, as if bad men decay into bad earth. Not all were executed, but all were criminals doing time. The memories here aren't happy, and few mourners leave flowers, much less celebrate wasted lives. Peckerwood Hill is little more than a 22-acre potter's field, since these dead prisoners had neither money nor family willing to claim their corpses.

Peckerwood Hill was an unused patch of private land when the new Texas prison in Huntsville mistakenly began using it as a burial ground in 1853. A couple of years later, the landowners deeded it to the State of Texas, reckoning a boneyard for scoundrels wasn't much use for anything else.

No burial records were ever kept, but photos of Peckerwood Hill in 1899 show many graves, all marked with wooden crosses, according to Jim Willett, the former prison warden who now runs the Texas Prison Museum in Huntsville. When it comes to death and prison, Willett is an indisputable expert: In three years as warden between 1998 and 2001, he witnessed eighty-nine executions, more than any warden in American history.

For its first hundred years, Peckerwood Hill was little more than an untended trash heap, spiritually and physically. Nobody cared much. Weeds and brush engulfed it, hiding graves while time and the elements rotted their wooden crosses. When Captain Joe Byrd organized the massive cleanup in the 1960s, he located 922 graves, although nobody knows exactly who's in 312 of them. Many more were lost forever.

Texas executed its first inmate (by electrocution) on February 8, 1924—followed quickly by four more within a few hours. Three of those five men are buried side-by-side on Peckerwood Hill.

Texas has executed more than 900 more inmates since 1924. Now as then, a grave is hand-dug by inmates, sometimes before there's a dead man to fill it. Funerals always begin at 8:30 a.m., and there might be two or three in short order. The dead convict is buried in his release clothes, a work shirt and khaki pants. He is transported by a proper hearse, not a state pickup. Four inmates act as pallbearers, then bury the casket after the death-house chaplain says a few words. Sometimes mourners come, sometimes they don't.

"We all die somehow," says former death row chaplain the Reverend Carroll Pickett, who led ninety-five men to their deaths between 1982 and 1997 and is now an ardent opponent of capital punishment. "A lot of these men were relieved to finally be done with it. If they believed in an afterlife, had any faith at all, this was freedom."

Among the notable buried here:

- Serial killer Henry Lee Lucas (GPS: 30.71222 / -95.53595), who killed at least five people—including his mother—and confessed controversially to hundreds. He partnered with transvestite-cannibal Ottis Toole in 1976, but they split up after Lucas started living with Toole's seven-year-old niece . . . who later turned up dismembered. Lucas's death sentence was commuted by Governor George W. Bush in 1998, and he died in prison of heart failure in 2001 at the age of sixty-four. His body was unclaimed.

- Serial killer Kenneth McDuff (GPS: 30.71237 / -95.53661) was the only man in American history to be assigned two death row numbers. After raping and murdering three teens in 1966, McDuff was paroled in 1989 to reduce prison crowding. In 1992 he was arrested for the murder of a twenty-two-year-old woman and implicated in three other murders. He was executed by lethal injection in 1998.

- Prison rodeo clown Lee Smith's (GPS: 30.71217 / -95.53750) epitaph reads, "At Rest, in Memory of Rodeo Pals." His

Thousands of criminals have been laid to rest at Texas's oldest and biggest prison cemetery, including nearly two hundred executed killers.

popularity apparently had its limits, though, because he was killed in 1941 while trying to steal another inmate's commissary treats.

- Peckerwood Hill's most famous "resident" busted out long ago. Kiowa chief Satanta, who was imprisoned in 1874 for leading insurgent raids on Texas settlers and inspired the character Blue Duck in Larry McMurtry's *Lonesome Dove*, committed suicide by leaping from a prison window and was buried on Peckerwood Hill in 1878. In 1963 his grandson claimed his bones and reburied them in Fort Sill, Oklahoma. A monument to Satanta remains (GPS: 30.71180 / -95.53690).

TEXAS PRISON MUSEUM
Huntsville

The museum is on the east side of I-45, off exit 118, just north of Huntsville. Open 10:00 a.m. to 5:00 p.m. Monday through Saturday, noon to 5:00 p.m. Sunday; closed major holidays. Admission charged. GPS: 30.735833 / -95.584444

If you want a wine museum, go to Sonoma County. If you want a movie museum, go to Hollywood. And if you want a prison museum, go to Huntsville, Texas. Established in 1989, this 10,000-square-foot museum explores the history of Texas's famous (or infamous) prison system since 1848.

The museum's centerpiece is the macabre Old Sparky, an electric chair handmade by inmates to electrocute 361 prisoners between 1924 and 1964. It was rescued from a prison trash dump after lethal injection became the preferred method of execution in Texas in 1982 and is displayed in a replica of the old Texas Death Chamber. Nearby are the tubes and straps used by Texas executioners in America's first-ever lethal injection and the ancient TWX Model 33 teletype machine that transmitted an unknown number of instant reprieves from the governor's office.

But it's not all about death. The rest of the museum features many historical exhibits about convict life. Among the novelties displayed are an old-fashioned ball-and-chain, a variety of creative weapons made by inmates (including a blackjack made from lead-paint chips pressed into a heavy ball and slung in a sock), and a superb assortment of shanks, fake guns, and digging tools. You can also walk into (and fortunately, out of) a replica prison cell.

You'll also see such marvelous artifacts as the hollow-heeled, drug-smuggling shoe worn by Texas murderer Charles Harrelson—actor Woody's father; a handgun retrieved from Bonnie and Clyde's death car; and a unique five-barreled shotgun made secretly by some inmates who planned to escape.

Prison Driving Tour

The Texas Prison Museum is the starting place for the Prison Driving Tour, which will lead you to the spot where all freed inmates catch a bus to points unknown; the old prison rodeo grounds; all eight prisons in Huntsville (including the Walls Unit, where the modern death chamber is housed); Sam Houston State University's Criminal Justice Center; and Peckerwood Hill. Pick up your map and brochure at the museum's front desk.

The museum's gift shop offers prisoner bobbleheads, crafts and leather goods made by inmates, and a chance to be photographed in prison garb. If you like to read, the bookstore also offers several excellent penology titles, including a history of Old Sparky titled *Have a Seat, Please.*

HATE-MURDER OF JAMES BYRD JR.
Jasper

Huff Creek Road, also known as CR 278, is west of Jasper, off FM 1408. The Jasper City Cemetery is on North Main Street, or GPS 30.931685 / -94.000772.

Walking home from a party in the wee hours of a summer night, James Byrd Jr. (1949–1998) was offered a ride by three local men, but their intentions were not charitable. The three—white supremacists John William King, Lawrence Brewer, and Shawn Berry—took Byrd, who was black, to dark and rural Huff Creek Road, where they beat him, stripped him naked, chained him by his ankles to a pickup truck, and dragged him 3 miles until his body literally disintegrated into grisly bits. The gruesomely sadistic trail of body parts began on a dirt logging road just past the Huff Creek bridge (GPS: 30.92795 / -93.90061) and ended where they dumped his grotesquely dismembered corpse near the Huff Creek Church, a little-used black chapel and cemetery (GPS: 30.93004 / -93.86775).

This hideous murder sparked a national wave of revulsion and reminded America that the specter of Jim Crow hadn't been erased from all hearts. Black Panthers and Ku Klux Klansmen gathered for separate rallies in front of reporters from all over the world. But

James Byrd Jr. was dragged to death behind a pickup down Huff Creek Road by white supremacists in 1998.

cooler heads in Jasper—both black and white—prevented further racial unrest.

All three killers were eventually convicted; King and Brewer are on death row, while Berry is serving a life sentence and is eligible for parole in 2038.

Byrd was buried in the Jasper City Cemetery on the black side of a fence that separated black graves from white (GPS: 30.92984 / -94.00185). But Jasper, wracked by the racist turmoil the murder caused, removed the fence in 1999. Basketball star Dennis Rodman offered to pay for Byrd's funeral but relatives declined the offer; instead, they accepted $25,000 to help support Byrd's family. His headstone has been desecrated more than once with racist graffiti and is now enclosed within an iron fence.

KILLER DICK DUBLIN'S DEATH SITE
Junction
The Texas historical marker is on US 377, about 9.5 miles south-west of Junction. GPS: 30.391391 / -99.89675

In 1878 four Texas Rangers led by the legendary James B. Gillett rushed the hideout of killer Dick Dublin and his gang about 60 yards east of this marker. Dublin ran and was shot by the Rangers. Other gang members were captured and later convicted of a mail robbery at Pegleg Station. The location of Dublin's grave is unknown. Gillett, who died in 1937 in Marfa, is a member of the Texas Ranger Hall of Fame.

VICTIM CHELSEA McCLELLAN'S GRAVE
Kerrville
Garden of Memories Cemetery is at 3250 Fredericksburg Road, on TX 16 about 3 miles northeast of Kerrville. The grave is in the Babyland section. GPS: 30.07856 / -99.10063

The 1982 death of blond and blue-eyed Chelsea McClellan, only fifteen months old, unmasked Genene Jones, a child-killing pediatric nurse who might have been involved in as many as fifty suspicious child deaths over four years at a San Antonio hospital. Chelsea's little body was exhumed in 1983, and new tests found a fatal dose of succinylcholine, a powerful muscle relaxer.

Jones was charged with Chelsea's murder and later with a second child's murder. Prosecutors successfully argued that Jones liked the attention and excitement the deaths brought her. She was convicted in both trials and sentenced to ninety-nine years in prison; she will be automatically paroled in 2017. Jones was not charged in any of the other suspicious deaths because the hospital shredded all records related to her employment and drug data.

This case spawned the 1983 book *Death Shift* by Peter Elkind and the 1991 TV movie *Deadly Medicine* starring Susan Ruttan.

TEXAS CHAINSAW MASSACRE HOUSE
Kingsland
Now the Junction House Restaurant, 1010 King Street, opposite the Antlers Hotel. GPS: 30.66013 / -98.43700

In 1973 a brash young director named Tobe Hooper filmed a little indie movie about a group of friends who journey to central Texas when they hear the Hardesty family cemetery has been vandalized. On the way, they stop at the old Hardesty mansion, where they come face-to-face with a cannibal family—including the chainsaw-brandishing Leatherface. Hooper filmed for only about four weeks around Austin, Bastrop, and Round Rock, where his crew found an old Victorian farmhouse on Quick Hill to portray the fictional Hardesty manse. Released in 1974, the blood-spattered *Texas Chainsaw Massacre* is hailed as one of the greatest horror flicks of all time.

The cult-favorite Texas Chainsaw Massacre *was filmed in this house.*

In 1998 the empty cult-film landmark was cut into seven pieces—one hopes with a chainsaw—and reassembled in Kingsland as a restaurant. It has served food under a few different names, but you won't see many clues to its slasher-movie past unless you go into the upstairs bathroom, where an original *Texas Chainsaw Massacre* movie poster hangs. But just to be safe . . . don't go in the freezer.

VICTIM HAZEL BROWN'S GRAVE
Knobbs Springs
The cemetery lies beside the Knobbs Springs Baptist Church, about 12 miles west of Lexington. Signs point the way to both along CR 305 south from FM 696. GPS: 30.36177 / -97.19830

Hazel "Schatzie" Brown (1916–1938) was a pretty country girl whose life was anything but idyllic. At fifteen she had her first child out of wedlock and soon left her son and family to make her way in the world. At nineteen she had another son out of wedlock in San Antonio and gave him up for adoption.

Fate caught up with Hazel when she took a job as a waitress at Joe Ball's Sociable Inn in Elmendorf, Texas—and disappeared. After the suspected killer Ball committed suicide rather than be arrested, a cohort revealed where he and Ball had dismembered Hazel's corpse and buried her body parts in a shallow grave. For fun, they tossed her severed head in a campfire. Police collected the twenty-two-year-old girl's remains and sent them back to Knobbs Springs, where they were buried in a family plot. In 1989 her first son died and was buried beside the mother who abandoned him.

Also see "Victim Minnie Gotthardt's Grave" (Aransas Pass), "Serial Killer Joe Ball's Grave and Tavern" (Elmendorf), and "Ranger Johnny Klevenhagen's Grave" (San Antonio).

"Best Little Whorehouse in Texas"

The Chicken Ranch in La Grange was drawing crowds for eighty years before it proved, in Hollywood terms, the entertainment value of lust.

Established in 1905, Miss Jessie Williams's brothel later moved from La Grange's red light district to 11 acres outside of this small farm town. The "ranch" got its name during the Great Depression, when Miss Jessie charged $1.50 for a sex act—but would accept a chicken as payment.

Miss Jessie ran a smart, tight ship. She demanded proper behavior of her girls and her customers, proclaiming proudly that she admitted politicians and cops but no drunkards. She patrolled her hallways diligently and chased off troublemakers with an iron rod.

During the World Wars her girls sent care packages to overseas soldiers—future customers. She kept the law at bay by forming a close relationship with the sheriff, who gleaned gossip and tips about criminals during his nightly visits.

As business boomed, Miss Jessie added haphazard rooms to the clapboard bordello until it was a cluster of carnal cubicles built around a reception parlor where visitors could play the jukebox and buy soft drinks and cigarettes. No drinking was allowed.

Confined to a wheelchair with arthritis in the mid-1950s, Miss Jessie left the daily operations to twenty-seven-year-old Edna Milton, a hustling young, um, hustler. After Miss Jessie died in San Antonio in 1961, Miss Edna bought the ranch from her heirs for $30,000 and immediately set out to bolster business with sixteen girls who saw from five to fifteen customers every day. Fifteen minutes of companionship cost $15. She forbade her girls from any social contact with the La Grange locals. Her prostitutes got weekly medical examinations, and all the ranch's supplies were bought from local stores.

More importantly, Miss Edna allowed Sheriff Jim Flournoy to install a direct phone line to the whorehouse so he could continue to gather intelligence about local crime. Flournoy fingerprinted and photographed all new girls, and anyone with a criminal past was dismissed.

Business exploded. Miss Edna's girls made $300 a week with no expenses, and in the 1960s the ranch was earning more than $500,000 a year. Men often waited in line on weekends, when college students and soldiers from nearby bases came a-callin'. Some say that one military base even transported officers to the Chicken Ranch by helicopter. And during the 1950s, a visit to the bordello became part of the initiation rites for many Texas A&M freshmen.

Things were finger-lickin' good at the Chicken Ranch until 1973, when a flamboyant, wig-wearing Houston TV reporter named Marvin Zindler aired a weeklong series about how the local sheriff had turned a blind eye to a well-known criminal enterprise operating openly in his county. Viewers were shocked and dismayed that Texas had a whorehouse in it. Shocked.

Public pressure mounted on Governor Dolph Briscoe, who ordered the Chicken Ranch closed. Flournoy and the local prosecutor carried a petition with 3,000 signatures to Austin, but to no avail. The Chicken Ranch was plucked.

Two Houston lawyers bought the ranch and moved the main house to Dallas, where it became the centerpiece of a funky chicken restaurant—with Miss Edna as hostess. The restaurant closed a year later, but in 1979 Miss Edna took a small, nonspeaking role in a new Broadway musical about the Chicken Ranch, called *The Best Little Whorehouse in Texas,* which twisted Miss Edna and Flournoy's unconventional business relationship into a romance. When she left Broadway, Miss Edna returned to obscurity in Texas.

Today only a crumbling husk of the Chicken Ranch remains at this hidden site just south of Rocky Creek Road, east of La Grange (GPS: 29.91335 / -96.83475). Thanks largely to the movie version of the musical,

Not much remains of the Chicken Ranch, celebrated on stage and in film and as "the best little whorehouse in Texas."

curious tourists often look for a magnificent Victorian mansion—but the Chicken Ranch was always just a modest farmhouse cobbled together with extra rooms, like a building inspector's worst nightmare. The spot is rich with decay and cow patties, showing signs of teen partying and the tenacity of cactus, which grows through the floorboards in some spots. This is private property, and the owners discourage trespassers.

Jim Flournoy resigned in 1980 after thirty-four years as sheriff of Fayette County, and he once declared he was tired of hearing about the Chicken Ranch. He died in 1982 at age seventy-seven, just as the movie version of *The Best Little Whorehouse in Texas,* starring Burt

Reynolds and Dolly Parton (as musical versions of himself and Miss Edna), was released. More than a hundred lawmen attended the funeral, where Flournoy was celebrated for solving every murder and bank robbery in his county for more than three decades. Inside the new La Grange City Cemetery, on the east side of North Travis Street, you'll find Flournoy's grave in the section that forms the southeast corner of A Avenue and Second Street (GPS: 29.90976 / -96.86661).

Muckraking Marvin Zindler died of cancer in 2007. Not long after the Chicken Ranch closed, he came to La Grange for a follow-up story and got into a shoving match with Sheriff Flournoy, who reportedly snatched Zindler's toupee and waved it around like a scalp. Zindler sued for $3 million and won a small out-of-court settlement. The late Dom DeLuise played cartoonish crusader Melvin P. Thorpe in the movie; for the record, Zindler loved the musical, hated the movie. He was buried in Houston's Beth Israel Memorial Gardens at 1101 Antoine Drive, between Hartland Street and Northampton Way (GPS: 29.78918 / -95.47626).

OUTLAW BILL WHITLEY'S GRAVE
Mahomet

Mahomet Cemetery is about 11 miles northeast of Bertram on Ranch Road 243 in Burnet County. GPS: 30.81588 / -97.93408

Like so many other Texas desperadoes, Bill Whitley (1864–1888) was a product of the turbulence of the post–Civil War South. His outlaw life began after his brother was killed by a lawman in 1884.

Barely twenty years old, Bill formed a gang to rob trains and at least one bank. In 1888 U.S. marshals and Texas Rangers foiled the Whitley gang's train robbery near Harwood, Texas, and chased the robbers for several days. When lawmen finally caught up with the gang near Floresville, Whitley was killed in the ensuing shoot-out. He was twenty-four.

After Whitley's body was publicly displayed in San Antonio, his wife, Cordelia, brought it back to Mahomet for burial. Upstanding local citizens protested, but Cordelia reportedly held a gun on several of them while Bill's friends dug his grave and lowered him into it.

DEAD MAN'S HOLE
Marble Falls

This isolated spot is 2 miles south of Marble Falls on US 281. Go a half-mile east on FM 2147 and then a half-mile south on CR 401 to the historical marker. GPS: 30.52843 / -98.264921

In the late 1860s some seventeen corpses—likely pro-Union locals—were found in this 160-foot-deep natural limestone hole, whose mouth is only about 7 feet wide. Only three were ever identified. A hanging tree that once grew over the hole is now gone. In the hot summer months, a foul odor emanates from the cave.

DEPUTY JOHN WHORLIE (OR WORLEY) DEATH SITE
Mason

The fatal well site and historical marker is near the corner of Westmoreland Street and Avenue F in Mason. GPS: 30.74865 / -99.24366

Deputy John Whorlie (1845–1875) was escorting suspected cattle rustler Tim Williamson to court when a lynch mob ambushed and killed Williamson during a range feud known as the "Hoodoo War." Scott Cooley, the dead rancher's adopted son and former

Texas Ranger, swore revenge on the killers—and one of his first targets was Whorlie, who he believed had conspired in the ambush. Cooley found Whorlie digging a water well, shot him in the head, then scalped him and threw his body into the hole. Today a historical marker stands at the well site, though Whorlie's body was eventually retrieved and buried in Mason's Gooch Cemetery (GPS: 30.75289 / -99.22198). Cooley was later jailed but soon escaped with his gunfighter friend Johnny Ringo.

Also see "Vigilante Scott Cooley's Grave" (Blanco).

TEXAS SLAVE RANCH
Mountain Home

The ranch's stone gate is on the north side of TX 27, about 2 miles north of the intersection with FM 479. This is private property. GPS: 30.15952 / -99.34653

Hitchhiking through a central Texas summer can be a bad dream, but in the 1980s getting picked up by one Texas ranch family turned into a nightmare.

Rancher Walter W. Ellebracht Sr. and his son, Walter Jr., lured hitchhikers to their ranch by promising jobs, but the unlucky ones who accepted the offer might have been forced into slavery—or worse. In 1984 frightened ranch hands told cops that at least a hundred such hostages had been tortured, killed, and shredded in a wood-chipper. Investigators found bits of human bone and cassette tapes of torture sessions in which a cattle prod was used to shock a man.

The Ellebrachts were eventually convicted on racketeering charges, including the murder of Anthony Bates, an Alabama drifter who worked for them and disappeared. Another worker testified that Bates's body was burned. District Attorney Ron Sutton, a small-town prosecutor who had just convicted serial killer Genene Jones, sought life sentences for the two, but the jury meted out comparatively soft punishments, possibly because the victim was a homeless vagrant. With the help of famous defense attorney Richard "Racehorse" Haynes, Walter Sr. got probation (and has since died), and his son served only three years of his fifteen-year sentence. The ranch was sold to pay legal bills.

The 2005 movie *Hoboken Hollow,* whose cast included Dennis Hopper, C. Thomas Howell, and Greg Evigan, was based on the Texas Slave Ranch case.

Serial Killer Dean Corll

The moldering, tortured corpses of several young boys almost certainly still lie in hidden graves throughout southeast Texas, where they were buried by a mild-mannered Pasadena electrician and former candy-maker named Dean Corll (1939–1973). After Corll's violent death in 1973, police found twenty-seven victims of this sadistic pedophile, but almost nobody believes his true death toll will ever be known.

Working in his mother's candy business after getting out of the military in 1964, Corll often offered free sweets to the children at a nearby grade school—and coworkers remember him digging odd holes where he claimed to be burying bad batches of candy. By 1970 the aging Corll employed two young "helpers" to trap his victims.

Corll's accomplices—teenage dropouts Wayne Henley and David Brooks—were paid at least $200 for each boy they lured to his house at 2020 Lamar Drive in Pasadena (GPS: 29.68139, -95.21394). Inside this modest, unremarkable home was a torture chamber, outfitted with a plank to which victims could be handcuffed, a large knife, ropes, bizarre sex toys, and sheets of plastic over the carpeted floor to deflect splattering blood. The room also contained a large wooden crate with air holes. Here, Corll's victims suffered unspeakably.

When Corll's sado-sexual urges were satisfied, the boys were strangled or shot, then their corpses were buried in secret mass graves on the beach at nearby High Island, near Lake Sam Rayburn, or in Corll's rented boat shed in southwest Houston (4500 Silver Bell Street, or GPS 29.63822 / -95.44830), where seventeen corpses were later found buried under the dirt floor in Stall No. 11.

It all crashed to a halt on August 3, 1973, when Henley brought two friends, including a girl, to Corll's house and an argument erupted. When it was over, Henley had shot Corll six times. The serial killer was dead.

Henley and Brooks both confessed to their roles in Corll's crimes and led police to the bodies. Henley (born 1956) is serving six consecutive life terms; Brooks (born 1955) got one life sentence. Corll, who had served only a year in the U.S. Army, was buried with military honors at Grand View Memorial Park in Pasadena (Lot 288, Space 5 in the Garden of Devotion, or GPS 29.66422 / -95.10683).

Soon after Corll's death, the term "serial killer" was introduced into our lexicon. With twenty-seven confirmed victims ranging in age from thirteen to twenty-one, Corll officially became the most prolific American serial killer until his body count was surpassed by John Wayne Gacy's thirty-three victims in 1978. But Corll's death toll is likely much larger; his accomplices insisted there were at least three more young victims unfound.

Seventeen of Corll's twenty-seven known victims were found buried in Stall 11 at this boat shed.

Houston police were widely criticized for abandoning their investigation when Corll's body count exceeded Juan Corona's record of twenty-five.

A suspected twenty-eighth victim was identified in 2009, but forty years later, two unidentified Corll victims remain in the Harris County Medical Examiner's cooler, never claimed. Efforts to identify them continue.

Corll became known as "The Candy Man," but in an ironic twist, a year later another Houston man, Ronald Clark O'Bryan, laced his children's Halloween candy with cyanide, killing one. O'Bryan became known as "Candy-man" and was executed in 1984.

Corll's sordid crimes were detailed in the classic true-crime book *The Man with the Candy* by Jack Olsen (Simon & Schuster, 1974).

RAPPER "BIG HAWK" HAWKINS'S GRAVE
Pearland

Paradise South Cemetery is at 16001 Cullen Boulevard, just south of Beltway 8 on Houston's south side. GPS: 29.56890 / -95.34933

Houston rapper John Edward "Big Hawk" Hawkins (1969–2006) had scored a No. 45 single on Billboard's rap charts, had two young sons, and had gotten married less than a month before he died in a drive-by shooting. The killing remains unsolved. In 1998 his younger brother, rapper "Fat Pat" Hawkins, was also shot to death and is buried nearby. That murder is also unsolved.

GRAVE OF ASSASSINATED JUDGE JOHN WOOD
Rockport

Rockport Cemetery is just north of the intersection of Picton Lane and Sorenson Drive in Rockport. The grave is in Section 17 of the cemetery's Old Part. GPS: 28.04597 / -97.037441

U.S. District Judge John H. Wood Jr. (1916–1979), descendant of Texas pioneers, became the first federal judge assassinated in the twentieth century when he was gunned down by a sniper in front of his San Antonio town house. His tendency to impose the maximum sentences against drug traffickers earned him the nickname "Maximum John." Wood was assassinated by freelance hit man Charles Harrelson—the father of *Cheers* actor Woody—on behalf of Texas drug lord Jimmy Chagra, who was awaiting trial in Wood's court.

Early in the Wood investigation, Harrelson also "confessed" to killing President Kennedy in 1963,

Judge Wood's assassination is mentioned in Cormac McCarthy's 2005 novel *No Country for Old Men*. In the film version, Woody Harrelson plays a hit man with a startling similarity to his own real-life father.

but later recanted (although many conspiracy theorists still think he was involved). He got a life sentence for Wood's murder and died of a heart attack at age sixty-eight in Colorado's "Supermax" federal prison in 2007.

A San Antonio school and the federal courthouse were later named for Wood. Texas native Harrelson's final resting place is unknown, but he once wished for his cremated ashes to be scattered over the John H. Wood Federal Courthouse.

VICTIM KATHY WHITMAN'S GRAVE
Rosenberg

Davis Greenlawn Cemetery is at the corner of US 59 North and FM 2218. The grave is in Section H, Space 5, Lot 42, beneath a live oak tree. GPS: 29.53707 / -95.77673

In 1962 Kathy Leissner (1943–1966) met a young marine named Charles Whitman at the University of Texas. After a whirlwind courtship they married in the Catholic church where the former Eagle Scout Charles had been an altar boy. But four years later, in the wee hours of August 1, 1966, Charles killed his own mother and then stabbed twenty-three-year-old Kathy to death as she slept in their bed.

Over the next few hours, Whitman wrote in his diary and amassed an arsenal of guns and ammunition before heading to the University of Texas Tower. During the coming daylight hours, the most infamous sniper in American history would kill fourteen more people and wound another thirty-one.

Whitman was killed by police during his attack and was buried at Hillcrest Memorial Park in West Palm Beach, Florida, in a joint funeral with his slain mother.

Also see "Texas Tower" (Austin).

OUTLAW SAM BASS'S GRAVE
Round Rock

Round Rock City Cemetery is on the north side of Sam Bass Road about a half-mile west of I-35. The grave lies against the cemetery's west fence, beside the slave section. GPS: 30.51759 / -97.69778

You might think Sam Bass (1851–1878) was a favorite son of Round Rock, where they've named a major road, a Little League, a community theater, and a fire department for him. But this young outlaw—made mythic by the dime novels of his day—did nothing more for Round Rock than die there during a botched bank robbery.

At age nineteen the Indiana-born orphan came to Texas, where he performed odd jobs and eventually won a little cash as the owner of a successful racehorse. But after his short-lived racing career slumped, he found riches by forming various gangs and robbing trains, stagecoaches, and banks throughout the West. Soon, Bass had the attention of both the popular press and the Texas Rangers.

In 1878, two years after the Bass gang's first real scores, Sam hatched a plan to rob the Williamson County Bank in Round Rock, but one of his cohorts snitched, and the Texas Rangers were waiting. Local deputy A. W. Grimes unwittingly (and fatally for him) set off a shootout when he approached the gun-toting strangers. Bass's chief lieutenant, Seaborn Barnes (1849–1878), was killed outright, another gang member fled, and Bass escaped, mortally wounded.

The next morning Bass was found alive in a nearby pasture and taken to a makeshift jail, where he died the next day—his twenty-seventh birthday. He and Barnes (aka Nubbins Colt) were buried together without fanfare beside the slave section of the Round Rock City Cemetery, but in time Bass would become one of Round Rock's most celebrated "citizens."

Over the years souvenir-hunters chipped away at Bass's limestone marker until it was almost gone. A modest new obelisk now marks his final resting place next to his "right bower" Barnes (who also has a new marker), but the nub of Bass's original gravestone lies just behind it. Bass's newest epitaph: "A brave man reposes here. Why was he not true?"

GRAVE OF LAWMAN A. W. GRIMES
Round Rock

Round Rock City Cemetery is on the north side of Sam Bass Road about a half-mile west of I-35. The grave is in the cemetery's northeast corner. GPS: 30.51836 / -97.69685

A former Texas Ranger, Deputy A. W. Grimes (1850–1878) knew the Sam Bass gang was coming to town to rob a bank, but maybe he didn't think the three gun-toting cowboys he challenged could possibly be the legendary outlaw and his men. But when the three came out of a mercantile near the local bank, he reminded them that carrying guns in Round Rock was illegal . . . so they shot him, setting off a bigger gunfight with Texas Rangers who had been waiting for them.

Townsfolk collected $200 for the twenty-eight-year-old Grimes's widow and three children and gave them one of the would-be robbers' horses, then buried Grimes less than 100 yards from his likeliest murderer, Sam Bass. His weathered original headstone bears the epitaph "Gone But Not Forgotten," although for more than a hundred years Grimes was essentially forgotten. While the town was naming a number of local landmarks for the outlaw Bass, it wasn't until 2000 that a street was named for Grimes.

FANNIE PORTER'S BROTHEL
San Antonio

The Boys Town building is at 503 Urban Loop, just inside I-35 on the west side of downtown San Antonio. GPS: 29.421217 / -98.5008

British-born Fannie Porter (1873–ca. 1940) was one of the Old West's most famous madams. By age fifteen she was a prostitute in San Antonio and by twenty, owned her own brothel, where her girls were known to be among the prettiest, cleanest, and best dressed. Her "sporting house" was a favorite of good guys and bad—and everyone in between. Among her girls were the legendary Etta Place, Laura Bullion, and Della Moore, all of whom later ran with Butch Cassidy's Wild Bunch, regular customers at Fannie's bordello.

Today the original structure—which became a Catholic convent after Fannie retired in 1914 and is said to be haunted—remains just beneath the stucco skin of the San Antonio Boys Town's current building. Urban Loop (formerly San Saba Street) was once a dirt road where Butch Cassidy gave Fannie rides on the handlebars of his bicycle—the inspiration for a famous scene in the 1969 film *Butch Cassidy and the Sundance Kid*.

Fannie eventually faded away and disappeared from history. Like many Old West legends such as Butch and Sundance themselves, her death is a mystery: She might have returned to England, or married a rich man, or died in an El Paso car crash in 1940, according to various legends.

Also see "Grave of Outlaws Ben Kilpatrick and Ole Hobek" (Sanderson) and "Outlaw Will Carver's Grave" (Sonora), both in chapter 5, and "Wild Bunch Photo Studio" (Fort Worth) in chapter 3.

BATTLE OF FLOWERS PARADE SHOOTING RAMPAGE
San Antonio
The site of the shooting is the corner of East Grayson Street and Broadway. GPS: 29.443408 / -98.476814

For more than 110 years, thousands have lined the streets of San Antonio for the Battle of Flowers parade, the biggest event in the city's ten-day spring Fiesta. But on April 27, 1979, one spectator wasn't there for the pageantry. Drug-addled and paranoid Ira

Attebery (1915–1979) parked his Winnebago at the corner of East Grayson Street and Broadway, buttressed its walls with rolls of paper towels, and arrayed an enormous arsenal of guns and ammo inside.

As the parade began, Attebery began firing from his motor home into the crowd. After thirty minutes of free fire, police fired tear gas into the RV and sixty-four-year-old Attebery shot himself in the head. Two women died, and about fifty other people—including more than a dozen children—were wounded. Attebery was buried in his hometown of Poplar Bluff, Missouri.

Dillinger Gang Sites

Some of the best-known gangsters of the 1930s shared more than a sociopathic distaste for the law . . . they also shared a little Jewish gunsmith in San Antonio.

It isn't known how Hyman S. Lebman (1903–1990) befriended hoodlum Lester Gillis, aka Baby Face Nelson, but by the 1930s Lebman was supplying Baby Face with Thompson submachine guns and full-auto conversions of many handguns. Through Nelson, many of these illegal weapons got into the arsenals of Al Capone, Pretty Boy Floyd, the Barker-Karpis gang, and Baby Face's buddies in the John Dillinger gang.

Baby Face and other Dillinger gangsters made several trips here for guns, often renting rooms at the posh downtown Aurora Hotel (509 Howard Street, or GPS 29.44136 / -98.49568). In 1933, on a gun-buying trip to San Antonio, Baby Face and his wife even shared Thanksgiving dinner with fellow gangster Homer Van Meter at Lebman's modest home in a peaceful, tree-lined

Gunsmith Hyman Lebman supplied illegal guns to many of the Gangster Era's most wanted outlaws.

neighborhood north of downtown (418 Fulton Avenue, or GPS 29.46159 / -98.50008).

During that same trip, after a local madam told cops some Chicago gangsters were in town, Dillinger cohort Tommy Carroll fled a downtown traffic stop and was cornered in an alley at 430 East Commerce Street (GPS: 29.423726 / -98.488086). Just as he was being surrounded by cops, Carroll whipped out two pistols and shot his way out of the jam, killing Detective Henry Perrow and wounding another. Carroll fled the blind alley and jumped on the running board of a passing car. He found his way to Lebman's gun store (111 South Flores Street, or GPS 29.42356 / -98.49451), where he changed clothes and escaped out the back. (Carroll eluded a San

Antonio manhunt but was killed by police in Waterloo, Iowa, six months later.)

In 1934, after G-men narrowly missed capturing or killing Dillinger and his gang at the Little Bohemia Lodge near Rhinelander, Wisconsin, they traced many of the gangsters' deadliest weapons to Lebman. He began to tell everything he knew. The gunsmith eluded federal charges, but he was convicted of breaking a state law against the sale and possession of machine guns—and his occasional troubles with the law would last for almost fifty more years because of his association with gangsters.

But Lebman outlived his famous customer and all his buddies. Baby Face Nelson was gunned down in Illinois almost exactly a year after his Thanksgiving dinner at Lebman's home, and Dillinger died in a police ambush on a Chicago street in July 1934. Dillinger cohort Harry Pierpont insisted right up to his October 1934 execution that his gang's unraveling began with the San Antonio shootout and Lebman's squealing.

Lebman died in 1990 at age eighty-seven. He was buried in the Agudas Achim Jewish Cemetery, which lies between Crockett, Potomac, Palmetto, and St. James Streets in the city's cemetery complex on East Commerce Street (grave is at GPS 29.42325 / -98.46447). Some of Lebman's modified guns are still displayed at the FBI headquarters in Washington, D.C.

Detective Henry Perrow is buried in the San Fernando Cemetery #3 at 1735 Cupples Road (grave is in Section 7, Lot 690, or GPS 29.38854 / -98.55485). The alley where he was slain by Tommy Carroll has been converted into an entrance to the San Antonio Riverwalk.

FATAL CORNER CRIME SCENE
San Antonio

The Fatal Corner is at the northwest corner of Commerce and Soledad Streets in downtown San Antonio. GPS: 29.425027 / -98.49315

San Antonio in the late nineteenth century was raw and wild, a snake's nest of roads and plazas, festooned with open-air vendors, outhouses, mule-drawn streetcars, uncollected manure, saloons, butcheries, drunk cowboys, poor peasants, and many outlaws. In 1872 a former Civil War hero and well-liked city cop named Jack Harris opened a new saloon that quickly became the most popular entertainment spot in town. Across the road from the Main Plaza, Jack Harris's Vaudeville Theater and Saloon's variety shows, gas-lighted tavern, gaming rooms, and sporting girls attracted everyone from common cowpunchers to famous outlaws such as Billy the Kid, Butch Cassidy, and John Wesley Hardin. The mix was volatile, and violence was common.

In 1882 Harris himself was killed by former friend Ben Thompson at the theater's front door, a murder avenged two years later when Thompson and drinking buddy King Fisher were gunned down by Harris's friends inside the theater itself. Those deaths and others etched this spot's nickname in blood: the Fatal Corner. In 1886 the theater burned down and was replaced by the Elite Restaurant and Hotel, where guests stayed in rooms that weren't numbered but known by state names (swells roomed in "New York" and rubes in "Arkansas"). A bank office building exists on the site today.

The front doorway where Thompson killed Harris faced Commerce Street, about 30 feet west of Soledad.

Also see "Oakwood Cemetery" (Austin), "Grave of Victim Jack Harris" (San Antonio), and "Outlaw King Fisher's Grave" (Uvalde).

TEXAS RANGERS AND BUCKHORN MUSEUM
San Antonio

The museum is at 318 East Houston Street. Open 10:00 a.m. to 5:00 p.m. daily (except holidays). Admission charged. GPS: 29.426366 / -98.488795

This 8,000-square-foot private museum opened in 2007 and is built around artifacts from the Former Texas Rangers Association, which operated its own museum starting in 1936. While not the official Rangers repository, it displays fascinating artifacts and breaks down the lawmen's history into three parts: pre–Civil War, post–Civil War, and Ranger Town, a walk-through exhibit. Rare holdings are displayed in the Special Exhibit room.

Also see "Texas Rangers Headquarters" (Austin) and "Texas Ranger Hall of Fame and Museum" (Waco, chapter 3).

VICTIM MARY BEA PEREZ'S GRAVE
San Antonio

San Fernando Cemetery #2 is at 746 Castroville Road, about 3.5 miles west of the downtown area. The grave is in Block 37, Section, 4, Space 16. GPS: 29.41503 / -98.55228

Nine-year-old Mary Bea Perez (1990–1999) disappeared from Market Square during Fiesta on April 18, 1999. A week later, her badly decomposed body was discovered in a downtown drainage ditch. Her murder remained a mystery for two years, until confessed serial killer Tommy Lynn Sells admitted to kidnapping and strangling her. Sells was already on Texas's death row for murdering a thirteen-year-old Del Rio girl when he pleaded guilty to Mary Bea's slaying. The sexual psychopath Sells, who tended to target children, has confessed to as many as seventy other murders over a twenty-year period.

In 2005 Mary Bea's family celebrated what would have been her *quinceañera*—a traditional coming-of-age ceremony on a Latina's fifteenth birthday—at her grave.

Also see "Val Verde County Judicial Center" (Del Rio, chapter 5).

CONFEDERATE CEMETERY
San Antonio

The cemetery is at the northwest corner of East Commerce Street and New Braunfels Avenue. GPS: 29.420633 / -98.463917

Also known as City Cemetery #4, this historic graveyard is just one of more than thirty in a vast necropolis east of the downtown area. It was officially established in 1885, although at least one grave here dates to 1855. Today more than 900 markers have been documented, including those for Civil War, World War I, and World War II veterans and their families. Here you'll find the graves of:

- George Wythe Baylor (1832–1916), a restless soul who failed to find gold in California but found his legacy as a hero of the Confederacy in the Civil War, a legislator, and a respected Texas Ranger. In 1881 he led a detachment of Rangers in the last Indian battle in Texas. He is a member of the Texas Ranger Hall of Fame and is buried in Section 3, Lot 45. (GPS: 29.420717 / -98.4639)

- John "Rip" Ford (1815–1897), former Texas Ranger and Confederate officer who earned his nickname during the Mexican-American War, when one of his tasks as a regimental adjutant was to report the daily tally of soldiers killed in action. Beneath his name on each report, he wrote "Rest in Peace"—but as the death toll climbed, Ford abbreviated it simply to "RIP." He is a member of the Texas Ranger Hall of Fame. (GPS: 29.41995 / -98.4637)

RANGER AND GUN DESIGNER
SAMUEL WALKER'S GRAVE
San Antonio

Odd Fellows Cemetery is at the northeast corner of North Pine and Paso Hondo Streets. GPS: 29.421283 / -98.4697

Samuel Walker (1817–1847) was a Texas Ranger, but his claim to fame is designing one of the most popular six-shooters in the Old West: the Walker Colt. This .44-caliber pistol was the most powerful handgun of its day and was widely used by both good guys and bad on the Texas frontier and in the Mexican-American War—where Walker was killed at age thirty in a battle with Mexican guerrillas. Samuel Colt reportedly said the enormous gun—16 inches long and weighing over four pounds—"would take a Texan to shoot it."

You get an added historical bonus for visiting Walker's grave: Local legend suggests he shares his plot with the charred remains of the Alamo defenders, which were allegedly exhumed from the spot where they were cremated by Mexican troops after the battle of the Alamo in 1836 and reburied at this site between Walker and fellow Texas Ranger R. A. Gillespie. The claim has never been verified—nor disproven.

GRAVE OF VICTIM JACK HARRIS
San Antonio

City Cemetery #1 is at 1301 East Commerce Street. GPS: 29.42 / -98.466917

Jack Harris (1834–1882) was a Civil War veteran and local cop who also happened to own San Antonio's most popular entertainment spot, Jack Harris's Vaudeville Theater and Saloon. In 1880 his old army buddy Ben Thompson—a noted ruffian and Austin saloonkeeper himself—made angry threats against Harris after losing a lot of money gambling at a table with Harris's dealer Joe Foster.

THE CRIME BUFF'S GUIDE TO OUTLAW TEXAS

Two years later, Thompson (now an Austin city marshal) came back to town and declared he intended to close down Harris's establishment, which occupied a notorious spot in downtown San Antonio known as the "Fatal Corner." Forewarned, Harris hid with a shotgun just inside the theater's doors as Thompson approached. In the resulting gunfight, Harris was shot through the heart, a killing for which Thompson was ultimately acquitted.

Brazenly, Thompson returned to the scene of his crime two years after the killing, even though he knew Harris's friends, especially Joe Foster, had vowed revenge. He and drinking buddy King Fisher died in a fusillade of bullets as they watched the vaudeville show. Thompson was buried in Austin and Fisher in Uvalde, and nobody was ever prosecuted in their murders.

Joe Foster (1837–1884) accidentally shot himself in the leg during the attack on Thompson and Fisher and later died of his wound. He is buried beneath a tall stone just behind Harris's grave. Harris's grave lay unmarked for a hundred years until a local group unveiled a new tombstone on the centennial of his murder.

Also see "Oakwood Cemetery" (Austin), "Fatal Corner Crime Scene" (San Antonio), and "Outlaw King Fisher's Grave" (Uvalde).

RANGER LEE HALL'S GRAVE
San Antonio

San Antonio National Cemetery is at 517 Paso Hondo Street. GPS: 29.42155 / -98.4667

Lee Hall (1849–1911) was a schoolteacher-turned-lawman. As a Texas Ranger and a fearless gunfighter, he trailed some of Texas's most infamous outlaws, such as Sam Bass, John Wesley Hardin, and King Fisher. He bore a special dislike for Ben Thompson, the Austin gunslinger-turned-marshal. Hall retired to run a Texas cattle ranch, where a sickly young man named William Porter lived for two years, collecting material for stories he would later write under his pen name, O. Henry. Hall, who died at age sixty-one, is a member of the Texas Ranger Hall of Fame.

Also see "O. Henry Museum and House" (Austin), "Outlaw Sam Bass's Grave" (Round Rock), "Outlaw King Fisher's Grave" (Uvalde), and "Outlaw John Wesley Hardin Sites" (El Paso, chapter 5).

"KING" CARRASCO'S DOWNFALL
San Antonio
Roselawn Cemetery is at 1735 Cupples Road. The grave is in Section 7, Lot 462. GPS: 29.38799 / -98.55428

As vicious as any drug kingpin before or after, Frederico Gomez "King" Carrasco (1940–1974) controlled much of America's heroin supply in the 1960s and '70s. The murderous mobster was arrested in a bloody shootout outside Room 110 at the El Tejas Motel (2727 Roosevelt Avenue, or GPS: 29.37372 / -98.48181) in 1973, and committed suicide a year later at the end of a historic eleven-day prison-break-gone-bad that left two female civilians among his fifteen hostages dead. He's buried in an unmarked grave at San Antonio's Roselawn Cemetery.

FORT SAM HOUSTON NATIONAL CEMETERY
San Antonio
The cemetery is at 1520 Harry Wurzbach Road. GPS: 29.476824 / -98.434314

Many notable graves can be found in this enormous national cemetery for military and their families.

- History buffs know the brave exploits of the frontier's Buffalo Soldiers, black cavalrymen who fought in the Indian Wars, but few know about the Buffalo Soldiers' most infamous hour. A few months after America joined

World War I, the U.S. Army's all-black 24th Infantry Regiment was sent to build military installations in Houston, where they immediately met a hostile reception from both black and white locals.

In August 1917 a white cop arrested a black soldier who interfered with the arrest of a drunken black woman, then pistol-whipped black Corporal Charles Baltimore when he was sent to investigate the fracas. The racial tension exploded. More than a hundred armed black soldiers stormed Houston's streets and rampaged for two hours. Fifteen whites and four blacks were killed in the riot.

The largest court-martial in American history quickly convicted one hundred enlisted black soldiers in the riot. Because it was wartime, punishment was swift and

Nineteen black soldiers were hanged for their role in a 1917 race riot, and seventeen eventually were buried in the Fort Sam Houston National Cemetery.

unforgiving. Nineteen were sentenced to die and sixty-three to life sentences. No civilians were prosecuted.

Thirteen of the mutineers—including Corporal Baltimore—were hanged in the predawn darkness at San Antonio's Camp Travis on December 11, 1917. They were buried in unmarked graves in mesquite scrub beside the temporary gallows (GPS: 29.464255 / -98.427474), a wooded spot now inside Fort Sam Houston. Almost a year later, six more mutineers were hanged in San Antonio. In 1934 and 1937 seventeen sets of remains were exhumed from their unmarked graves and reburied at Fort Sam Houston National Cemetery. Today those executed soldiers lie in a single row starting with Corporal Baltimore's grave (Section P-A, Space 36, or GPS 29.47742 / -98.43269). Two sets of remains were returned to the mutineers' families.

Two of the five policemen killed in the riot are known to be buried in Houston. Shot and bayoneted by the mob of black soldiers, Ira Raney (1878–1917) was buried at Evergreen Cemetery (GPS: 29.73827 / -95.32145) and Daniel Patton (1888–1917) was buried in Hart-Singleton Cemetery (GPS: 29.79818 / -95.25385).

- Austin policeman Billy Paul Speed (1943–1966) was eating lunch in a nearby cafe on August 1, 1966, when he heard gunshots coming from the Texas Tower. The twenty-two-year-old 82nd Airborne veteran crouched behind a stone wall on the campus mall, but sniper Charles Whitman shot him when he peeked out. He was the only lawman killed that day. (Plot X, 2948, or GPS 29.47723 / -98.42978)

- Al Gratia (1920–1991) was an Army Air Corps crewman during World War II, but he was killed at age seventy-one when he rushed deranged gunman George Hennard during his rampage at the Luby's Cafeteria in Killeen, Texas, on October 16, 1991. Al's wife, Ursula (1924–1991), was shot to death a few minutes later and is buried with him. In all, twenty-three innocent people were killed in America's deadliest shooting spree at the time. The Gratias' daughter Suzanna, who was licensed to carry a gun but was prohibited by Texas law from carrying it into the restaurant that day, escaped with minor injuries and later won a seat in the Texas Legislature on the strength of her passionate campaign in favor of civilian gun rights across the USA. (Plot 18, 0, 65, or GPS 29.47359 / -98.43043)

- Actor Glenn Corbett (1933–1993) was neither a cop nor a robber . . . but he played them on TV. In a career that lasted more than forty years, the Korean War vet appeared in such crime fare as *Police Story*, *Petrocelli*, *The Rockford Files*, and *Gunsmoke*. He also played Sheriff Pat Garrett in the 1970 film *Chisum*, although he's best known as Linc Case from *Route 66*. (Plot Q, 0, 138-AM, or GPS 29.47607 / -98.43011)

RANGER JOHNNY KLEVENHAGEN'S GRAVE
San Antonio

Mission Burial Park South is at 1700 Southeast Military Drive. The grave is in Block 10, Lot 165. GPS: 29.344917 / -98.465067

Johnny Klevenhagen (1912–1958) wanted to be a policeman so badly that he lied about his age and became a San Antonio motorcycle cop at age seventeen. From there he worked his way up to the Texas Rangers, building a reputation as a tenacious sleuth who wouldn't shoot unless somebody shot at him. He investigated several major Texas cases, including the killings of serial killer Joe Ball, who likely fed his victims to pet alligators behind his Elmendorf tavern, and the cleaning up of organized crime in Galveston.

Klevenhagen, who died of a heart attack at age forty-six, is a member of the Texas Ranger Hall of Fame.

Also see "Victim Minnie Gotthardt's Grave" (Aransas Pass), "Serial Killer Joe Ball's Grave and Tavern" (Elmendorf), and "Victim Hazel Brown's Grave" (Knobbs Springs).

TEXAS "BODY FARM"
San Marcos

Located on the 4,200-acre, university-owned Freeman Ranch, just off CR 213, a few miles northwest of San Marcos. For obvious reasons, the site is not open to the public. GPS: 29.93329 / -97.99795

The largest of only three such "body farms" in the United States, Texas State University's 10-acre Forensic Research Facility studies human decomposition for clues to help criminal investigators determine when and how people died. At the facility, modeled after Dr. Bill Bass's literally groundbreaking "body farm" at the University of Tennessee–Knoxville, forensic anthropology students measure decay under different scenarios, such as being buried at different depths, in vehicles, underwater, and in varied Southwestern weather conditions and seasons. Up to six corpses (all willed to the school) are being studied at any given time, and the facility offers regular training to death investigators.

The ranch was bequeathed to Texas State University by the estates of Joe and Harry Freeman, wealthy Texas entrepreneurs. If you wonder whether they'd approve of their ranch being used, in part, to study decaying bodies, don't fret: J. Edgar Hoover was a frequent visitor, and for many years the Freemans hosted annual FBI deer hunts. For proof, read the inscription on the flagpole in front of the ranch house: "Presented to Mr. Joe and Harry Freeman in grateful appreciation by their FBI friends on the occasion of the 20th Annual FBI Hunting Party, November 1967."

The body farm is off-limits to all but approved visitors. It is protected by high-tech security devices within two high fences, and the ranch managers are fairly good shots. In other words, don't try to sneak in . . . unless you've willed your recently dead body to forensic science.

SITE OF SHERIFF PAT GARRETT'S FORMER HOME
Uvalde
The site is located roughly at 926 West Main Street/US 90. GPS: 29.202667 / -99.804667

One of the Old West's most famous lawmen, Pat Garrett (1850–1908) might—or might not—have killed Billy the Kid in New Mexico, but he definitely had some Texas ties. As a young man, he worked as a cowboy and a regulator on a Texas cattle ranch, and after he reportedly killed Billy the Kid, he became a Texas Ranger and a U.S. Customs agent in El Paso.

Legendary lawman Pat Garrett

This plaque marks the site of Garrett's home in Uvalde from 1891 to 1900, while he was raising racehorses with his partner, John Nance Garner, the future vice president under Franklin D. Roosevelt. Garrett eventually moved back to New Mexico, where he was murdered by old foes at age fifty-eight; future Teapot Dome schemer Albert Fall successfully defended Garrett's confessed killer.

Also see "Grave of Ollie Roberts (aka Billy the Kid)" (Hamilton, chapter 3) and "Evergreen Alameda Cemetery" (El Paso, chapter 5).

NEWTON GANG'S GRAVES
Uvalde

Hillcrest Cemetery is on US 90 on the western end of Uvalde. GPS: 29.2002 / -99.8122

In the interlude between the Old West outlaws and Depression-era gangsters, four sons of a Texas sharecropper became America's most prolific bandits. Between 1919 and 1924 the Newton Boys of Uvalde, Texas—Willis, Joe, Doc, and Jess—robbed more cash from American banks and trains than the Wild Bunch, Bonnie and Clyde, the Daltons, the James Gang, and John Dillinger *all put together.*

Like most outlaws before them, they sought the best life for the least effort, but the world was changing, and the Newton Boys put progress to good use. Instead of riding horses, they drove sleek cars. They didn't shoot open the locks on strongboxes, but instead used small amounts of nitroglycerine to crack bank vaults. And they didn't ride into town guns blazing, but rather often spent days formulating plans to snatch their loot and be long gone by the time anyone noticed.

Willis was the ringleader, but his brothers were eager followers. Before their five-year run ended, they had robbed six trains and almost ninety banks in a dozen states—two in one night in Hondo,

Texas! In 1921 alone, they stole at least $200,000, and throughout their criminal careers, not a single person was ever killed, a matter of considerable pride to the brothers.

The Newton Boys' masterpiece was the $3 million robbery of a mail train at Rondout, Illinois, in 1924, the biggest train robbery in American history. Doc Newton was accidentally shot by "friendly fire" during the heist, and federal agents soon caught up with Willis, Joe, and the ailing Doc in Chicago. But Jess escaped back to Texas with about $35,000 in loot. Fearing he'd soon be caught, too, he got drunk and buried the cash beside a rural road somewhere near San Antonio and marked the spot with a white stone—but he forgot the exact location, and the money has never been found. In time all four brothers negotiated lighter prison sentences with a promise to give all the money back—though they came up about $100,000 short.

After doing their time, the Newton Boys scattered but didn't necessarily go straight. Willis and Doc became bootleggers in Oklahoma and Missouri. Later, Willis and Joe were imprisoned for an Oklahoma bank robbery they probably didn't commit. In 1968 seventy-seven-year-old Doc was arrested for an attempted bank robbery, and in 1973 eighty-three-year-old Willis was implicated in a Texas bank robbery.

Eventually the Newton Boys all came home to Uvalde. Jess worked on local ranches until he died of lung cancer at age seventy-three in 1960. In 1974 Doc died of cancer at age eighty-three. The flamboyant Willis farmed with his wife, Louise, until he died at age ninety in 1979. Joe, a lanky cowboy who'd ride every year in Uvalde parades to great applause, died in 1989 at age eighty-eight.

In death, as in life, the Newton Boys stuck together. Willis, Jess (a World War I veteran), and Doc are buried beside each other and a fifth brother, Tull; Joe's grave is across the adjacent dirt path about 25 yards northwest of his brothers.

- Jess (1886–1960): GPS 29.200233 / -99.812217

- Doc (1891–1974): GPS 29.200233 / -99.812217

- Willis (1889–1979): GPS 29.2002 / -99.8122

- Joe (1901–1989): GPS 29.200217 / -99.8125

The brothers' exploits were depicted in the 1998 film *The Newton Boys*, starring Matthew McConaughey (Willis), Skeet Ulrich (Joe), Ethan Hawke (Jess), and Vincent D'Onofrio (Doc). Coincidentally, McConaughey was born in Uvalde.

Also see "Double Bank Robbery" (Hondo).

OUTLAW KING FISHER'S GRAVE
Uvalde

Pioneer Park is at the intersection of North Park and Florence Streets. GPS: 29.21525 / -99.792983

King Fisher (1854–1884) is one of the many Old West figures who rode on both sides of the law. A cattle rustler and gambler, this proud gunslinger was accused (but never convicted) of eleven murders—"not including Mexicans," he once proclaimed—before he was appointed a deputy sheriff in Uvalde County, soon becoming the acting sheriff.

In 1884 Fisher and his old buddy Ben Thompson, an equally notorious gunfighter who'd become an Austin city marshal, were assassinated by friends of Jack Harris, a San Antonio theater owner killed two years earlier by Thompson. Fisher, who was riddled by thirteen bullets, was originally buried on his ranch, but in the 1930s his body was moved to Uvalde's Pioneer Park. For many years the mother of one of Fisher's victims would visit his grave on the anniversary of her son's death and dance around a fire she built on it. Today a wrought-iron fence protects the site.

Also see "Oakwood Cemetery" (Austin) and "Fatal Corner Crime Scene" (San Antonio).

FOREST PARK EAST CEMETERY
Webster
The cemetery is at 21620 Gulf Freeway/I-45 at exit 25, west of the freeway. GPS: 29.51488 / -95.12177

- If you worry about poisoned Halloween treats, blame Ronald Clark O'Bryan (1944–1984). In a 1974 scheme to collect $20,000 in insurance money on his two children, Houston optician O'Bryan put cyanide in Pixy Stix candies and gave them to his kids and some neighborhood trick-or-treaters. O'Bryan's eight-year-old son, Tim, died, but miraculously, the other children never touched the tainted candy. O'Bryan, who became known as "Candyman," set off a nationwide wave of Halloween safety measures that are still used today. He was sent to death row, where he was executed by lethal injection in 1984; a small crowd of college students wearing Halloween costumes showed up to cheer as he died. O'Bryan's grave is at GPS 29.51675 / -95.12465. His son, Timothy, is buried in a Houston cemetery, Forest Park–Lawndale (GPS: 29.71296 / -95.30671).

- Another filicidal parent, Andrea Yates (born 1964), shocked America in June 2001 when she drowned her five children, aged seven months to seven years, in a bathtub. The former nurse had grown psychotic and suicidal after her first four children, then plunged deeper after the fifth was born. She explained the killings by saying she wasn't a good mother,

Andrea Yates drowned her five children in a bathtub in 2001, inspiring a national discussion about postpartum depression.

that the children were "not developing correctly," and she believed she should be punished for her shortcomings as a parent. Her 2002 life sentence for murder was overturned on appeal, and a 2007 jury found her not guilty by reason of insanity. She remains in a mental institution. Her biblically named children—Noah, John, Paul, Luke, and Mary—were buried together here in a funeral that drew hundreds of mourners. Their faces are poignantly etched on the large tombstone. (GPS: 29.51503 / -95.12365)

• Thirteen-year-old James Dreymala (1959–1973) was the last of twenty-eight known victims of sexual sadist and serial killer Dean Corll. He had been lured to Corll's Pasadena apartment, slaughtered, and buried secretly with other corpses in a Houston boat shed. The last to disappear, James was the first to be found. (GPS: 29.51519 / -95.12373)

Also see "Serial Killer Dean Corll" (Pasadena).

WORLD'S LUCKIEST MARSHAL'S GRAVE
Wharton

Wharton City Cemetery is on the 600 block of East Caney Street. The grave is under a tree. GPS: 29.310091 / -96.092885

Marshal Walter W. Pitman (1884–1935) was likely the luckiest lawman ever to wear a badge. In 1932 he escaped a chance shoot-out with Bonnie and Clyde with nary a scratch, but that wasn't his luckiest moment by far.

In 1917 Pitman tried to arrest a local drunk, who drew a .38-caliber pistol and began firing. Pitman fired back and, amazingly, his first bullet went into the drunkard's pistol muzzle and jammed his gun, enabling Pitman to arrest him. Fifteen years later *Ripley's Believe It or Not!* featured Pitman's incredible shot and he became famous. The drunkard's jammed gun remains to this day in the Ripley's archives in New York City.

Pitman's luck ran out in 1935 when he died of a massive heart attack while dragging another drunk to jail. He was only fifty-one.

Also buried in this cemetery is Pulitzer Prize–winning playwright Horton Foote (1916–2009), who won an Oscar for his screen adaptation of Harper Lee's *To Kill a Mockingbird.*

GRAVE OF RANGER PETE ROGERS
Woodville

Magnolia Cemetery is on the west side of North Dellius Road. Turn north off TX 190 at the First Methodist Church and go 3½ blocks. Cemetery is on the left. GPS: 30.78078 / -94.42273

World War II fighter pilot James Frank "Pete" Rogers (1922–1978) won three Distinguished Flying Crosses and twelve Air Medals before joining the Texas Rangers. He pioneered the Rangers' use of aircraft as a crime-fighting tool . . . oh, and helped quell a historic eleven-day prison siege in Huntsville that killed two female hostages. Two of the three inmates who tried to escape, including Texas drug kingpin Fred Carrasco, were killed, too.

Also see "'King' Carrasco's Downfall" (San Antonio).

2

BONNIE AND CLYDE

Whether it's their tragic story of star-crossed (and twisted) love or the public's insatiable hunger for sensational crime news, Bonnie and Clyde have captivated outlaw buffs for more than eighty years. The fascination is so enduring that two major books about them were published in 2009—seventy-five years after their violent deaths.

Bonnie and Clyde are the most recognizable names in Texas crime history, and their two-year criminal career was enough to spawn a mythology much larger than the reality of their exploits. It's nearly impossible to wander the back roads of northeast Texas without hearing dozens of family legends—some true—about the crooks. If all the "Bonnie and Clyde slept here" stories were true, their nights together would add up to far more than they enjoyed.

But in truth, the infamous lovers were neither Depression-era Robin Hoods nor particularly successful hoodlums. Their existence was bleak and their real lives insignificant, except to their victims. They were just two wild kids on a screaming tear, derided by contemporaries such as John Dillinger and Pretty Boy Floyd. In other words, the romance of Bonnie and Clyde was all in our minds.

Bonnie Parker and Clyde Barrow, both raised in poor parts of Dallas, met there in January 1930. Bonnie was only nineteen and married to a convict, but she fell hard for the swaggering, uneducated Clyde, a twenty-one-year-old small-time crook. Not long after they met, Clyde went to jail on a burglary charge but escaped with a gun Bonnie smuggled to him under her dress. Alas, Clyde was recaptured and stayed in jail until February 1932, when his love affair—and crime spree—with Bonnie really blossomed.

*Bonnie and Clyde's legend has been longer
lived than their short, bloody criminal career.*

According to the FBI, over the next two years they were linked to thirteen murders, several small-time robberies (what self-respecting desperado robs a fruit stand?), car thefts, and burglaries, and at least three kidnappings. Photos of them appeared in newspapers, and yarns about their exploits, not always accurate, gave them a can't-look-away cachet.

The Barrow Gang had a fluid membership. Gunmen Raymond "Elzie" Hamilton and Ralph Fults were with them for a while in 1932, then replaced by W. D. Jones. Clyde's brother Buck joined after he was released from prison in 1933, but was mortally wounded a few months later in an Iowa shootout. Trying to rebuild the gang in 1934, Bonnie and Clyde busted five convicts out of the Eastham State Prison Farm near Weldon, Texas, including Ray Hamilton, Joe Palmer, and Henry Methvin—a Louisiana kid who'd betray them nearly five months later.

Before sunrise on May 23, 1934, a posse of six Texas and Louisiana lawmen led by Texas Ranger Frank Hamer set a trap on a rural road near Gibsland, Louisiana, where Bonnie and Clyde were expected to pass. When the outlaws stopped their car later that morning, the posse opened fire without warning, killing Bonnie and Clyde instantly.

BARROW FILLING STATION SITE
The site is at 1221 Singleton Boulevard (called Eagle Ford Road at the time) in Dallas. GPS: 32.778658 / -96.841911

Clyde Barrow grew up in the back of his father's Dallas filling station. ROBIN JETT COLE

With money from an insurance settlement, Clyde's father, Henry Barrow (1874–1957), went from sharecropper to filling-station owner. The station sold gas, groceries, and other sundries, while the family lived in adjoining rooms behind. After Clyde's death, the house and station were fire-bombed a few times in a still-simmering feud between the Barrows and their son's old acquaintances.

ONE-TIME HIDEOUT

The River and Grocery Market building is at 200 North Burnett Street in Wichita Falls. GPS: 33.916862 / -98.502672

The outlaw couple reportedly hid out in the old River and Grocery Market building (built in 1925) when visiting Wichita Falls. An old wooden staircase on the east side led to six upstairs boarding rooms that shared a bathroom and tiny kitchen. Later the upstairs was converted into a bordello, and more recently it was a barbecue joint.

KEMP CALABOOSE

Located across the alley from the Kemp Police Department, 304 South Main Street in Kemp. GPS: 32.44097 / -96.23128

In April 1932 Bonnie, Clyde, and Ralph Fults were spotted burglarizing a hardware store in the small town of Mabank. When their stolen getaway car got bogged down in a swampy creek bottom, they rustled some mules and another car, but the pursuing posse caught up. In the ensuing shootout, a muddy Bonnie and the wounded Fults were captured, but Clyde escaped (a fact that peeved Bonnie). The two, using aliases, were thrown in this one-room, dirt-floored "calaboose" at Kemp until they were moved the next day to a proper jail nearby. Bonnie was never charged (Fults got five years), but it was reportedly the first night she ever spent in jail.

Bonnie Parker spent her first night in jail at this small-town hoosegow.

LILLIE McBRIDE HOME
The house is at 507 South Winnetka (formerly County Avenue) in Dallas. This is a private home. GPS: 32.741056 / -96.841958

After Clyde and Ray Hamilton robbed the Home Bank of Grapevine in January 1933, cops followed them to the home of Hamilton's sister, Lillie McBride. In the resulting shootout, Clyde killed Tarrant County deputy Malcolm Davis near the front porch.

EASTHAM STATE PRISON FARM
Located at 2665 Prison Road #1, 13 miles west of Trinity on FM 230 in Houston County and about 25 miles north of Huntsville. GPS: 30.9755 / -95.6336

Clyde was sentenced in 1930 to fourteen years at the notoriously tough Eastham State Prison Farm, where inmates did hard labor under the supervision of brutal guards. Clyde's 1932 escape plan was simple: He had another inmate chop off two of his toes so he wouldn't have to work. He was sent back to the main prison in Huntsville where, ironically, he was paroled only days later with a limp he'd have for the rest of his short life. In 1934 Bonnie and Clyde raided Eastham to spring several gang members, killing a guard in the headlong escape. Prisoners still work the farm today.

Bonnie's legal husband, a convicted killer named Roy Thornton (1908–1937), was shot here during an escape attempt just a few years after Bonnie died. He is buried in the prison cemetery, which is closed to the public. After Bonnie's death, Thornton told a reporter, "I'm glad they went out like they did. It was much better than getting caught."

STOCKYARDS HOTEL

The hotel is at 109 East Exchange Avenue, in Fort Worth's Stockyards area (800-423-8471). GPS: 32.788912 / -97.348786

Ask for Room 305: Bonnie and Clyde spent a night there in 1933. Or so hotel flaks claim.

RED RIVER PLUNGE

The site is just west of where US 83 crosses the Salt Fork of the Red River, about 6 miles north of the Panhandle town of Wellington. GPS: 34.567009 / -100.195827

In 1933 Bonnie Parker, Clyde Barrow, and gang member W. D. Jones were speeding toward a Barrow Gang reunion in Oklahoma when their stolen Ford plunged off a washed-out bridge into the bank of the Red River near Wellington, Texas. Clyde and Jones were thrown clear, but Bonnie was stuck under the car when it burst into flames. As the fire began to sear the skin of her left leg, she cried out to be shot and put out of her misery. Luckily, two local farmers arrived to help extricate Bonnie and took her back to a nearby farmhouse (GPS: 34.95551 / -100.21969) to treat her burns.

When two local cops came to investigate a report of armed strangers, a melee erupted and Jones shot one of his rescuers' daughters, young Gladys Cartwright, in her thumb. Clyde then kidnapped the lawmen and stole their car, with the gravely wounded Bonnie on the backseat. Clyde later freed the cops in Oklahoma and took Bonnie to a doctor, who said she was near death. She recovered, but the burn scars were noted in her autopsy a year later.

The farmhouse where Bonnie and Clyde were taken after the wreck—and where they took their hostages—is now a tumbledown heap just east of the historical marker on northbound TX 83 (GPS: 34.95576 / -100.22100). The plaque repeats misinformation that Clyde's brother Buck was there, but eyewitnesses merely assumed Jones was Buck.

The old bridge's northern abutment (GPS: 34.95755 / -100.22284) still exists at the rest area on the north bank, just west of TX 83. It was replaced in 1939 by a steel-truss bridge, which might soon be replaced itself.

A loaded pistol clip and one of Bonnie's leather gloves were retrieved from the wreckage and are displayed today at the Collingsworth County Museum, 824 East Avenue in downtown Wellington (GPS: 34.8553 / -100.21298).

Despite her famously scarred thumb, Gladys Cartwright outlived the entire Barrow Gang by decades. She died in 2006 at age ninety-six and is buried in Wellington's North Fairview Cemetery on FM 38. Her grave is in Section C, Lot 37.

TWO STATE TROOPERS MURDERED

The site is at the southeast corner of Dove Road and West Northwest Parkway in Grapevine. GPS: 32.970257 / -97.157544

On April 1, 1934, a black Ford V-8 with yellow wheels parked on a side road caught the eye of three passing motorcycle cops. When they stopped to help, Clyde and cohort Henry Methvin opened fire with a sawed-off shotgun and an automatic rifle, killing patrolmen Edward Wheeler and H. D. Murphy. Clyde, Bonnie, and Methvin then escaped, leaving the dead cops in the dirt road. A memorial marker was erected at this site but has been removed recently for road construction.

Wheeler is buried in Dallas's Grove Hill Memorial Park (GPS: 32.79210 / -96.72020) and Murphy is at the Old Palestine Cemetery near Alto, Texas (GPS: 31.65704 / -95.01077).

BONNIE PARKER'S GRAVE

Crown Hill Memorial Park is at 9700 Webb Chapel Road in Dallas. GPS: 32.86743 / -96.86393

Like her lover Clyde, Bonnie Parker (1910–1934) grew up poor. She was a decent student and loved to write poetry, but she had a penchant for bad boys. Her husband went to prison for murder in 1929, but she never divorced him and wore his wedding ring right up until she was killed in 1934 (it remains in the Parker family). Although she might never have actually killed anyone, Bonnie lovingly nurtured her and Clyde's mythology, sending newspapers a copy of her infamous poem, "The Story of Bonnie and Clyde," in the last few weeks of her life.

At twenty-three, Bonnie died in the passenger seat of Clyde's stolen tan Ford V-8 (now owned by a casino in Primm, Nevada), with a box lunch and a pistol on her lap and $6 in her purse. Her body had been hit by about forty bullets. Posse member Ted Hinton later wrote: "I see her falling out of the open door, a beautiful and petite young girl who is soft and warm, with hair carefully fixed, and I smell a light perfume against the burned-cordite smell of gunpowder, the sweet and unreal smell of blood."

Twenty thousand gawkers mobbed the mortuary where Bonnie's body was displayed. Her mother, Emma (1861–1952), refused to allow her to be buried beside Clyde. At Bonnie's funeral the day after Clyde's, planes dropped flower petals from the sky over the West Dallas Fishtrap Cemetery. In the 1940s, after her headstone had been stolen several times, Bonnie's grave was moved to Crown Hill Memorial Park, where her mother was also buried.

Her epitaph:

As the flowers are all made sweeter by
the sunshine and the dew, So this old
world is made brighter: by the lives
of folks like you.

CLYDE AND BUCK BARROW'S GRAVES
Western Heights Cemetery is at 1617 Fort Worth Avenue in Dallas. GPS: 32.76567 / -96.84663

For $500, twenty-five-year-old Clyde Barrow (1909–1934) was buried at sunset beside his outlaw brother Buck in a small, private service . . . surrounded by thousands of onlookers and hucksters. Some ghoulish souvenir-hunters had even tried to cut off Clyde's fingers and an ear. One entrepreneur offered Clyde's parents $50,000 for the outlaw's corpse, hoping to mummify it for carnival tours.

Clyde's bullet-ravaged body had been identified by the missing toes he had had chopped off in prison and the tattoos with old girlfriends' names *Anne* and *Grace* on his arm. Barrow Gang member Joe Palmer, a prison escapee who was being hunted, is said to have viewed the body at the mortuary without being recognized.

Parents Henry and Cumie Barrow and another Barrow brother, Elvin, are also buried beside Clyde and Buck. Today this cemetery is rarely open to the public and warns against trespassing. Clyde's headstone has been stolen several times.

GROVE HILL MEMORIAL PARK

Several Bonnie and Clyde figures are buried in this cemetery at 4118 Samuell Boulevard, Dallas, on the south side of I-30.

- Blanche Barrow (1911–1988) married Clyde's brother Buck in 1931 and persuaded him to surrender, but soon after his parole, they joined up with Bonnie and Clyde again. She was with the gang when they killed two policemen in Missouri, and while fleeing, was caught in an Iowa ambush. Buck was mortally wounded and Blanche was blinded in one eye by shattered glass. After serving her parole, she remarried and lived a law-abiding life. In 1968 Estelle Parsons won the best supporting actress Oscar for playing Blanche in the movie *Bonnie and Clyde*, but Blanche hated the film, which, she said, "made me look like a screaming horse's ass." She died a week shy of her seventy-eighth birthday and was buried under her married name, Blanche B. Frasure (Section H, or GPS: 32.79103 / -96.72002).

> Legendary Texas Ranger Frank Hamer (1884–1955), who led the six-man posse that violently ended Bonnie and Clyde's criminal careers in Louisiana, was buried in Austin's Memorial Park Cemetery. (See "Ranger Frank Hamer's Grave," Austin, chapter 1.)

- Kid-criminal Ralph Fults (1911–1993) accomplished something no other Barrow Gang member did: He lived to a ripe old age. His first arrest was at age fourteen, and by the time he joined up briefly with Bonnie and Clyde at age twenty, he was a hardened criminal. Convicted in a 1935 robbery, Fults was pardoned in 1954 and quit his outlaw ways by becoming a security guard at an orphanage, where he lectured kids about the evils of crime. He was the subject of a 1996 book about his criminal past, *Running with Bonnie and Clyde: Ten Fast Years of Ralph Fults*. Fults survived three prison escapes, multiple gunshots, high-speed chases, several car crashes, stabbings, and prison beatings, and died in Dallas at the age of eighty-two on March 16, 1993. His grave is in the Lawnview section (GPS: 32.78580 / -96.71893).

- Dallas Deputy Bob Alcorn (1897–1964) was one of six lawmen who ambushed Bonnie and Clyde on May 23, 1934, near Gibsland, Louisiana. He knew them on sight and was posted as a hidden lookout on the road. "We let him have it," he said a few hours after the surprise attack that pumped a deadly fusillade into the death car. Alcorn died at age sixty-six on May 23, 1964, the thirtieth anniversary of the ambush. His grave is in the Masonic section (GPS: 32.79083 / -96.71844).

- Three of Clyde's sisters—Artie Barrow Keys, Nell Barrow Francis, and Marie Barrow Scoma—are also buried in this cemetery.

GANG MEMBER JOE PALMER'S GRAVE
San Jose Burial Park is at 8235 Mission Road in south San Antonio. The grave is in Block H, Section 1, Lot 331. GPS: 29.34601 / -98.47452

In January 1934 Bonnie and Clyde orchestrated a deadly prison break from the Eastham State Prison Farm to free buddy Joe Palmer (1902–1935), Ray "Elzie" Hamilton, and other gang members. During the daring escape, Palmer killed a prison guard. Later convicted of the murder, Palmer was asked by the judge if he had a preference of an execution date. "Yes," he said, "make it 1999." His request was denied, and Palmer was executed in Texas's electric chair on May 10, 1935, the same night as Hamilton. Hamilton was so upset by the prospect of his electrocution that Palmer volunteered to go first.

Palmer was so popular with his fellow prisoners that they took up a collection to bury him next to his mother in San Antonio instead of Peckerwood Hill, Huntsville's dreary prison cemetery.

GANG MEMBER RAY HAMILTON'S GRAVE
Tiny, hidden Elmwood Memorial Park is at 8004 Scyene Avenue in Dallas. The grave is in Row 8. GPS: 32.76295 / -96.68431

Only 5-foot-3 and 120 pounds, Raymond "Elzie" Hamilton (1914–1935) was big enough to be Clyde's right-hand man. He and his brother Floyd ran with the Barrow Gang for a while, then broke off because Ray didn't think Bonnie and Clyde were ambitious

Bonnie and Clyde Artifacts

The Texas Ranger Hall of Fame and Museum (I-35 and University Parks Drive, 100 Texas Ranger Trail in Waco; www.texasranger.org) displays several artifacts from the Bonnie and Clyde ambush, including the guns used to kill them, weapons confiscated from the death car, Clyde's pocket watch, and the pistol found on Bonnie's lap. (See "Texas Ranger Hall of Fame and Museum," Waco, chapter 3.)

enough. Some historians also believe he was part of a sexual three-some with the outlaw couple. After repeated escapes, killings, and bank robberies, Hamilton was sentenced to 362 years in Huntsville prison and executed on May 10, 1935, right behind fellow gang member Joe Palmer. His last words: "Well . . . goodbye all."

GANG MEMBER W. D. JONES'S GRAVE

Brookside Memorial Park is at 13401 Eastex Freeway in Houston. The grave is in the Garden of the Apostles, St. Matthew section, Lot 468, Space 3. GPS: 29.91313 / -95.31544

W. D. Jones (1916–1974) ran with Bonnie and Clyde for a time, but after Buck Barrow was killed in a shootout, Jones decided the outlaw life was too dangerous. He bailed out on the gang and came home to Texas, where he was soon arrested. Jones, however, claimed he had been held captive by the gang, literally tied down at night to prevent an escape. He served a short prison stretch and disappeared . . . until 1968, when he sued Warner Brothers for what he called a "libelous" portrayal of him in the film *Bonnie and Clyde*. The suit was thrown out, but he told *Playboy* magazine he had merely been Clyde's "dupe." In 1974 the lifelong doper Jones was killed at age fifty-eight by a shotgun blast during a drug deal gone bad.

GRAVE OF LAWMAN TED HINTON

Sparkman Hillcrest Memorial Park is at 7405 West Northwest Highway in north Dallas. The grave is in the Acacia section. GPS: 32.86881 / -96.77759

Dallas Deputy Ted Hinton (1904–1977) knew Bonnie and Clyde better than any cop because he grew up with them in West Dallas, and he was assigned to track them over much of their brief, two-year crime spree. Clyde's father reportedly once told Hinton,

"Ted, I know you're going to have to shoot my boy." When he died at age seventy-three, Hinton was the last surviving player in the fatal 1934 ambush. His firsthand account, *Ambush: The Real Story of Bonnie and Clyde,* was published after his death. His son "Boots" Hinton opened a small museum in Gibsland, Louisiana, where he sells little swatches of bloody fabric from Clyde's death trousers.

Further Reading About Bonnie and Clyde

- *Bonnie and Clyde: The Lives Behind the Legend,* by Paul Schneider (Henry Holt, 2009).

- *Blanche Barrow: My Life with Bonnie and Clyde,* edited by John Neal Phillips (University of Oklahoma Press, 2004).

- *Go Down Together,* by Jeff Guinn (Simon & Schuster, 2009).

- *The Strange History of Bonnie and Clyde,* by John Treherne (Stein and Day, 1984).

3

NORTH TEXAS

FIRST NATIONAL BANK OF ALBANY
Albany

The bank building is at 100 South Main Street, on the west side of the street. GPS: 32.724503 / -99.297556

Jimmy Lucas (1912–1998) was a small-time Texas hood when he and a buddy robbed this little bank at high noon on July 18, 1934. Only twenty-two, the veteran bandit Lucas had escaped a month earlier from a Texas prison where he was doing time for a string of minor robberies. Both men were arrested after a high-speed chase and gun battle. But the $10,000 robbery in Albany is not what made Lucas famous.

Convicted in 1935, Lucas became Inmate No. 224 at the new Alcatraz Island prison in California, along with such notable thugs as Alvin Karpis, Doc Barker, Machine Gun Kelly, and a guy he hated—Al Capone. On June 23, 1936, Lucas sneaked up behind Capone and stabbed him with a pair of shears he had filched from the prison barbershop. Capone wasn't seriously injured, but Lucas (who reportedly went bonkers after spending six months naked in a pitch-black, clammy isolation cell) became a legend overnight.

A year later, Lucas and two other convicts tried unsuccessfully to escape the inescapable Rock, one of only fourteen attempts in the prison's twenty-nine years. In the chaos, Lucas killed a janitor and was eventually sentenced to life. But when Alcatraz closed in 1963, Lucas was freed. He died in Sacramento, California, at age

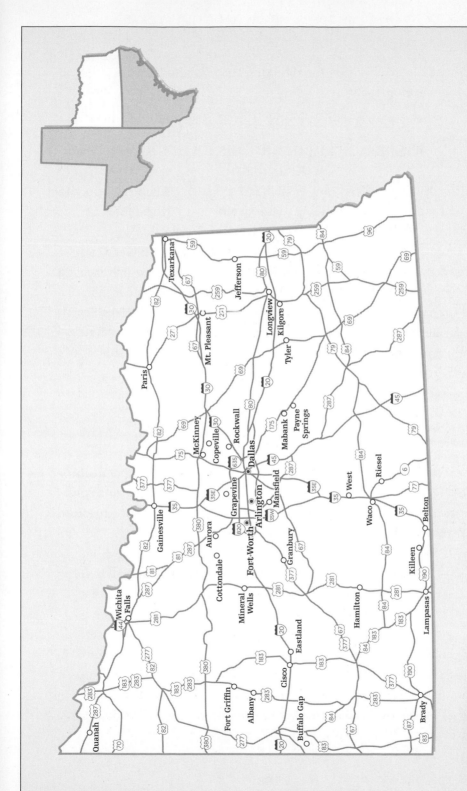

North Texas

eighty-six—still famous for shanking the fearsome Scarface . . . and living to tell about it.

KILLER CHARLIE BROOKS JR.'S GRAVE
Arlington

Cedar Hill Memorial Park is at 8301 US 287 (Business), on the north side of the highway. The grave is in Hope B, Lot 26, Space 5. GPS: 32.61475 / -97.18176

An accidental pioneer, Charlie Brooks (1942–1982) was the first American to die by lethal injection and the first to be executed in Texas in eighteen years when he went to the Huntsville death house on December 7, 1982, for tying up and shooting a young Fort Worth auto mechanic during a 1976 auto theft. Yet for all his history-making, Brooks lies in an unmarked grave on the right side of his mother, Berrie Brooks.

MOORE MEMORIAL GARDENS
Arlington

The cemetery is at 815 Randol Mill Road. Recently the cemetery stopped disclosing grave locations and prohibited any photography by unrelated visitors, except with family permission. Cemetery GPS: 32.75038 / -97.11792.

- Nine-year-old Amber Hagerman (1986–1996) was snatched while riding her bike in 1996. Four days later, her nude, molested body was found 4 miles away in a dry creek bed. Her murder remains unsolved, but it inspired the creation of Texas's Amber Alert system, which became a national program in 2003. To date more than 500 abducted children have been recovered alive because of Amber Alerts. Her grave is at GPS 32.75459 / -97.11712

- Heavy-metal guitarist Darrell "Dimebag" Abbott (1966–
  2004), former frontman for the popular band Pantera, was
  among four people shot by a deranged fan during a 2004
  nightclub concert in Columbus, Ohio. A cop then killed
  the shooter. Abbott's father is Jerry Abbott, a country-
  and-western songwriter and producer. (GPS: 32.753889 /
  -97.119722)

*Rocker Darrell Abbott was killed by a
deranged fan during a concert.*

SERIAL KILLER RICKY LEE GREEN'S GRAVE
Aurora

Aurora Cemetery is on the east side of Cemetery Road, about a half-mile south of TX 114. Green's grave is under a tree in the back left corner. GPS: 33.05382 / -97.49966

Blaming his bloodlust on a grotesquely abusive childhood, Ricky Green (1960–1997) was executed by lethal injection for castrating and fatally stabbing Steven Fefferman in 1986, but he killed at least three other people—two women and a sixteen-year-old boy—and was suspected in at least eight more bloody murders. He was caught after his estranged wife told cops she had helped the psychopathic Green in two of the killings. She was later convicted for her part but got only ten years' probation. *Blood Rush* by Patricia Springer (Pinnacle, 1994) delved into Green's crimes.

Aurora Cemetery is famous for a different burial, though. In 1897—six years before the Wright Brothers' first flight—a strange, cigar-shaped airship reportedly crashed on a local farm. In the wreckage, searchers found a small, humanlike creature they called "the Martian pilot." The little alien was given a proper Christian burial beneath a headstone engraved with a triangle or three circles (nobody's sure), but the marker has long since disappeared. In the 1970s investigators wanted to exhume the alien's corpse, but the Aurora Cemetery Association successfully thwarted them. Today legend suggests the little guy is buried beneath a contorted live oak tree (GPS: 33.05261 / -97.50067) near the center of the graveyard. (Of course, another legend claims he survived the crash, learned to drink whiskey and play poker, and was assassinated by the Texas Rangers.)

PRISON WORK WAGON DISPLAY
Belton

The wagon is on the north side of the Bell County Sheriff's Office and Jail, 111 West Central Avenue. GPS: 31.05681 / -97.46476

This wagon, which looks like something out of a spaghetti western, really transported county inmates to and from chain-gang projects in the 1800s.

MASS-MURDERER GEORGE HENNARD'S HOUSE
Belton

The house is at 301 East 14th Avenue. GPS: 31.068405 / -97.455592

This sprawling, four-bedroom brick mansion (private property) is where mass-murderer George Hennard lived when he went on a 1991 shooting rampage, killing twenty-three innocent people and himself at a Luby's Cafeteria in nearby Killeen. It was the deadliest shooting spree in modern American history until the Virginia Tech slayings. The house belonged to his absentee mother, and at the time of the shootings, the jobless Hennard was openly angry that it might be sold.

Also see "Luby's Cafeteria Massacre Site" (Killeen).

MURDERED RANGER STAN GUFFEY'S GRAVE
Brady

Rest Haven Cemetery is on US 283 just west of downtown Brady. GPS: 31.14335 / -99.35178

In 1987 Texas Rangers cornered desperate parolee Brent Beeler, who had kidnapped Kara-Leigh Whitehead, the two-year-old daughter of a Horseshoe Bay rancher. Beeler demanded a car and $30,000 in exchange for the little girl's life. Rangers Stan Guffey and John Aycock volunteered to hide in the back of the car to capture the kidnapper. The car was delivered, but Beeler quickly realized he'd been trapped. He shot Guffey before he was killed by Aycock, but the little girl was rescued unharmed. More than 750 mourners attended Guffey's funeral.

Sadly, the entire Whitehead family was killed in a 1992 plane crash.

CANNONBALL COURTHOUSE
Buffalo Gap

The courthouse is at 133 North William Street. Hours are 10:00 a.m. to 5:00 p.m. Monday through Saturday, noon to 5:00 p.m. Sunday. Admission charged. GPS: 32.28596 / -99.82787

Not immodestly, Buffalo Gap called itself the "Athens of the West" when this courthouse was built in 1879. Its most unique feature? The limestone block walls were mortised to contain cannonballs salvaged from Civil War battlefields to discourage inmates from chiseling their way out of jail. It is listed on the National Register of Historic Places.

SANTA CLAUS BANK ROBBERY
Cisco

The former bank building still stands at 708 Conrad Hilton Boulevard, or GPS: 32.388629 / -98.97954)

What better disguise at Christmas than Santa Claus? That's how freshly paroled Marshall Ratliff (ca. 1899–1929) dressed up to rob the First National Bank in Cisco (two days before Christmas in 1927). Unfortunately, it wasn't merry: Two cops were killed and six bank customers wounded in the violent holdup and resulting shootout. More than 200 bullet holes were later counted in the bank.

Sparking the largest manhunt in Texas up to that time, Ratliff and his gang were captured a week later and eventually convicted of murder and bank robbery; Ratliff got ninety-nine years. A year later, while facing more charges in Eastland County, he killed a jailer in a failed jail break (210 West White Street, or GPS: 32.40277 / -98.81919), so the frustrated citizens of Eastland decided to hurry justice. They snatched Ratliff from his cell and lynched him in a vacant lot behind the local Majestic Theater on Mulberry Street. When the first knot slipped, they did it again. Locals have erected

Marshall Ratliff robbed a bank disguised as Santa Claus, but when he tried to escape from this Eastland jail, a lynch mob wasn't feeling jolly.

a marker and fence around a utility pole behind the theater (190 North Mulberry Street, or GPS 32.40250 / -98.81982), but it's not clear if this is the actual death-pole.

Ratliff's mother claimed his body and buried him at Fort Worth's Mount Olivet Cemetery (2301 North Sylvania Avenue; the unmarked grave is in the David Crockett Lawn, Lot 333, Space 2. GPS: 32.79431 / -97.31286). His death certificate lists the cause of death as "hanging by the neck with a rope by mob."

Cisco's nondescript, one-story First National Bank building still stands and features a historical marker, some newspaper clippings, and historic photos from the time of the robbery. The Eastland jail Ratliff escaped from is now a local lawmen's museum that displays the rope used to lynch Ratliff.

"TEX" WATSON'S CHILDHOOD HOME
Copeville
The house is at 5578 TX 78. This is private property. GPS: 33.07936 / -96.41947

Charles Manson's right-hand man, Charles "Tex" Watson, grew up in this modest, three-bedroom bungalow. His father supported the family working at a service station next door (GPS: 33.07961 / -96.41926).

Watson was an honor student and star athlete in school, and was deeply involved in the Copeville Methodist Church (GPS: 33.08040 / -96.41552). After a couple of hard-partying college years in Denton, he headed to California, where he picked up a hitchhiker—the Beach Boys' Dennis Wilson—who introduced him to a guy named Charlie Manson. Eventually Watson became Manson's most trusted lieutenant in a sinister cult known as "The Family," which believed in an impending violent revolution it called "Helter Skelter."

To spark the revolt, Manson ordered the slaughter of several wealthy people in Los Angeles on two nights in 1969, and Watson led the grotesque killings of actress Sharon Tate, Leno and Rosemary LaBianca, and four others. Watson was arrested a few months later in Texas and fought extradition to California for nine months while jailed at the Collin County Prison. He was ultimately convicted of seven murders, but his death sentence was commuted to life in prison when California briefly abolished the death penalty in 1972.

While in prison, Watson was allowed to marry and fathered four children. He became a born-again Christian and formed his own continuing prison ministry, Abounding Love Ministries. Like other Manson Family members, Watson occasionally comes up for parole. Many books have covered Watson's part in Manson's crimes. He wrote one himself: *Will You Die for Me?* (Fleming H. Revell Co., 1978).

Also see "Collin County Prison" (McKinney).

GEORGE "MACHINE GUN" KELLY'S GRAVE
Cottondale

From FM 2123, go south on School House Road about 500 feet to an unmarked county road heading west. Cottondale Cemetery sits behind the white chapel building and work sheds about 500 feet west of School House Road. Kelly's small, flat marker lies on the right side of the central walkway in the center of the graveyard. GPS: 33.06479 / -97.70732

Like John Dillinger, Pretty Boy Floyd, and Bonnie and Clyde, George "Machine Gun" Kelly earned his place in the pantheon of American outlaws during the 1920s and '30s. The Tennessee-born bootlegger, bank robber, and kidnapper reportedly got his nickname from his second wife, Kathryn, a shrewd (and shrewish) Lady Macbeth who bought him his first tommy gun and became his partner in crime. In fact, it was Kathryn who coined the gangster term "G-man."

George and Kathryn's biggest crime was the 1933 kidnapping of Oklahoma oil millionaire Charles Urschel, whom they hid in a clapboard farmhouse owned by Kathryn's parents, Robert "Boss" and Ora Shannon, near Paradise, Texas. When the $200,000 ransom was paid, Urschel was released, but the FBI wasn't satisfied. Convicted in the first test of the new Lindbergh Law making kidnapping a federal offense, George and Kathryn got life sentences, and Kathryn's parents went to prison, too. Many outlaw historians agree the convictions marked the end of the Gangster Era.

After twenty-one years at Alcatraz, George died of a heart attack at Leavenworth Federal Penitentiary in 1954 on his fifty-ninth birthday. With nobody else to claim the body, Boss Shannon, George's father-in-law, allowed him to be buried in a family grave in this rural cemetery. Kathryn was offered a prison furlough to attend the funeral, but she refused, saying, "Just dig a hole and throw him in it." Kelly's headstone is a small, cheap, hand-lettered concrete marker that misspells his name as "Kelley." Two years later, Boss Shannon (1877–1956) was buried a couple of spaces north (GPS: 33.06488 / -97.70731).

Kathryn (1904–1985) and her mother served their time together before being paroled in 1958. In 1985 Kathryn died at age eighty-one and is buried in Tecumseh, Oklahoma, beside her ex-con mother, Ora (1888–1980), under the alias Lera Cleo Kelly.

The Paradise farmhouse no longer exists, but it's worth noting that to date, $100,000 of the Urschel ransom money has never been recovered.

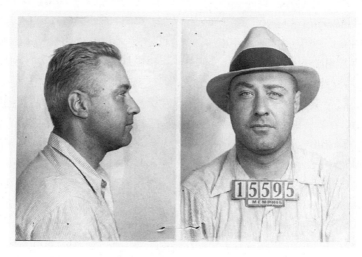

George "Machine Gun" Kelly

NEAR-VICTIM PRISCILLA DAVIS'S GRAVE
Dallas

Sparkman Hillcrest Memorial Park is at 7405 West Northwest Highway in north Dallas. The grave is in the northwest corner of the Garden of Eternity. GPS: 32.86739 / -96.78362

Estranged wife of wealthy oilman T. Cullen Davis, Priscilla Lee Davis (1941–2001) was the likely target of a 1976 murder attempt that instead killed her boyfriend and her twelve-year-old daughter. Her husband was acquitted of the killing, but Priscilla died of breast cancer in 2001 at age sixty. Her epitaph: "Explain not. Friends don't need it, enemies won't believe it."

Also see "Oilman Cullen Davis's Former Mansion" (Fort Worth).

GRAVE OF LAWMAN JOHN DUNCAN
Dallas

Greenwood Cemetery is at 3020 Oak Grove Avenue, near downtown Dallas. The grave is in Block 24, Lot 26, Space 11. GPS: 32.80185 / -96.79699

Ranger-turned-bounty-hunter John Riley Duncan (1850–1911) is most famous for helping arrest gunfighter John Wesley Hardin in Florida. Soon after, he quit the Rangers for more lucrative bounty-hunting. He was killed in a car crash near Dallas. No photos exist of Duncan, who believed they might inhibit his undercover work, but his tombstone proudly proclaims "Got Wes Hardin."

Also in Greenwood Cemetery: Dallas mayor Benjamin Long (1838–1877), who was killed when he tried to stop three people from leaving a local saloon without paying. Some votes just aren't worth it. (GPS: 32.80061 / -96.79659)

OUTLAW DOC SCURLOCK'S GRAVE
Eastland

Eastland City Cemetery is at 400 South Halbryan Street. The grave is at GPS: 32.397783 / -98.812533

Josiah Gordon Scurlock (1850–1929) was a leader of the Lincoln County Regulators, vengeful vigilantes in the New Mexico range war. Billy the Kid was their most famous member. Scurlock might have studied medicine in Louisiana, but "Doc" wasn't a doctor. Instead, he was a vicious gunfighter until New Mexico Governor Lew Wallace—author of *Ben-Hur*—pardoned all the Regulators, except the Kid. That's when Doc moved to Texas, where he gave away his guns, took a job with the highway department, and allegedly wrote book reports for University of Texas students before dying of a heart attack at age seventy-nine.

In the 1988 Hollywood western *Young Guns*, Scurlock was played by Kiefer Sutherland.

For details about the sensational events in Eastland and nearby Cisco related to the 1927 Santa Claus holdup, see "Santa Claus Bank Robbery" (Cisco).

SHAUGHNESSY'S SALOON
Fort Griffin

The old town site, known as "The Flat," is adjacent to the Fort Griffin State Historic Site, 1701 North US 283, 15 miles north of Albany. GPS: 32.932817 / -99.229117

One of the Old West's most famous friendships was forged on this spot when saloon owner and former boxer John Shaughnessy (1848–1919) introduced Wyatt Earp—a budding lawman on the trail of a train robber—to gambler John "Doc" Holliday. A legendary romance started here, too: This is where Doc Holliday met his prostitute-girlfriend, "Big Nose Kate" Horony.

When Wyatt Earp was introduced to Doc Holliday at Shaughnessy's Saloon, one of the Wild West's most famous friendships began.

This replica is built on the old saloon's original foundation. Private owners have re-created the town's old jail and other historic buildings in their original spots, too.

OILMAN T. CULLEN DAVIS'S FORMER MANSION
Fort Worth

The mansion is at 4100 Mockingbird Lane, off Stonegate Boulevard, in southwestern Fort Worth. GPS: 32.712453 / -97.382126

This twenty-room mansion on 180 acres was the site of an unsolved double murder in 1976—but police are no longer searching for the killer.

The home was built by oilman T. Cullen Davis in 1972, but by 1976 he and his wife, Priscilla, were embroiled in an untidy divorce and she was living in the mansion with her boyfriend and daughter. On August 2, 1976, a masked intruder killed the boyfriend and Priscilla's twelve-year-old daughter and wounded Priscilla. Three witnesses described Davis as the shooter, but he was eventually acquitted of killing his stepdaughter (he was never prosecuted for the boyfriend's killing). In 1978 Davis was tried again for allegedly hiring a hit man to kill Priscilla and the judge in his divorce case; again he was acquitted.

Davis sold his mansion in 1983, and since then it has been a church, a restaurant, and a banquet hall. Davis still lives somewhere in North Texas; Priscilla died of breast cancer in 2001 and is buried in Dallas's Sparkman Hillcrest Memorial Park (GPS: 32.86739 / -96.78362).

Two books and a Hollywood movie have been produced about the Davis case, reportedly the most expensive murder investigation and prosecution in Texas history.

SERIAL KILLER H. H. HOLMES'S PROPERTY
Fort Worth

The property is at the southwest corner of Second and Commerce Streets, a couple of blocks southeast of the Tarrant County Courthouse. GPS: 32.755971 / -97.331352

Although he wasn't America's first serial killer (as some have said), Herman Mudgett (aka Dr. H. H. Holmes) was certainly among our most ghastly psychopaths, well before tales of blood and gore became commonplace, prime-time entertainment.

The smoothly seductive swindler Holmes (1860–1896) admitted to 27 murders, but his toll could be more than 200. Much of his dirty work happened in a three-story Chicago hotel he built for the 1893 World's Columbian Exposition. Holmes's "murder castle" featured a second-floor labyrinth of guest rooms—some of which had been outfitted as "asphyxiation chambers," where guests could be suffocated with lethal gases. Other iron-clad rooms had blowtorch-like devices fitted into the walls.

The top floor had a coffin-size safe, soundproof rooms, and a chute that could deliver corpses to the basement, which held a bloody dissecting table, a torture rack, a crematory with a rolling grate to slide bodies into the fire, acid vats, and a pit filled with quick-lime. Down there, Holmes even hid a ball of his victims' hair.

In 1893 Holmes met a young Texas heiress named Minnie Williams, who believed Holmes (he told her his name was Harry Gordon) was a rich inventor. They were soon engaged to be married. Minnie lived at Holmes's horrific "castle" for more than a year and even came to know about her fiancé's crimes—maybe even participated in them.

Minnie inherited a valuable piece of Fort Worth property from a rich uncle, and she soon deeded it to one of Holmes's henchmen. And then during a visit to Chicago, Minnie's sister, Nannie, also signed over her share of the Fort Worth property—then disappeared forever.

Minnie soon disappeared, too. Holmes claimed she'd gone broke, had a bastard child (or an abortion), and might have committed suicide, but her remains were never found. Minnie's keepsake watch, however, was later found in the ashes of Holmes's crematory. Many people believe Minnie and Nannie were killed and their signatures forged on the stolen deeds.

When suspicions rose in Chicago, Holmes fled to Fort Worth, where he planned to build another "murder castle" on the Williams sisters' inherited property at Second and Rusk (now Commerce) Streets. In the 1890s many mansions dotted this upscale neighborhood, but today the area is part of Fort Worth's city center, no longer a residential district.

Holmes built his new three-story, brick horror house on the southwest corner. After his arrest, when the American public became fascinated with his first-person newspaper accounts of his killings, police searched the unfinished Fort Worth house. They found many of the same features as his Chicago "murder castle": a chute from the third floor to the basement, a room with twelve different doors, a modified sewer main, a man-size wooden box, and other "curiosities."

Oddly, it was horse-rustling, not murder, that undid Holmes in Texas. After Pinkerton detectives discovered he shipped a railcar of stolen horses to Chicago, Holmes and his party fled Fort Worth before the new castle was finished. They remained fugitives until Holmes was arrested in 1894 for killing his henchman in a Pennsylvania life-insurance scam. In 1896 Holmes was hanged and buried in an unmarked grave 10 feet deep under a ton of concrete in suburban Philadelphia's Holy Cross Cemetery.

H. H. Holmes is a central figure in the true-crime book *The Devil in the White City* by Erik Larson (Random House, 2003).

THE WINDSHIELD MURDER
Fort Worth
The crime scene is at 3840 Wilbarger Street. GPS: 32.70007 / -97.266487

A drunken, drug-addled Chante Mallard was driving to her Fort Worth home on a late October night in 2001 when her car hit Gregory Biggs (1964–2001), a homeless man. The impact hurled him through Mallard's windshield, his head inside the car and his broken legs flailing on the hood. Mallard, a nurse's aide, drove home with Biggs stuck in her broken windshield.

She parked in her one-car garage, apologized to the crying man who was bleeding profusely, then went inside to have sex with her boyfriend. Police say Biggs lived for two days lodged in Mallard's windshield and might have been saved if rushed to a hospital. With the help of friends, Mallard later dumped his mangled corpse near some playground equipment in Cobb Park (GPS: 32.70918 / -97.29902) and torched the seats in her car. She was arrested four months later, after she told a friend at a party, "I hit this white man"—then giggled.

Convicted of murder in 2003, Mallard got a fifty-year sentence. She is eligible for parole in 2027.

This dreadful crime was fictionalized in the 2007 horror film *Stuck,* inexplicably starring Mena Suvari (who's white) as the Chante Mallard character (who's black). And how's this for a Hollywood happy ending? In the film the Biggs character escapes and burns his would-be killer and her boyfriend to death.

HISTORIC OAKWOOD CEMETERY
Fort Worth
Oakwood Cemetery is at 701 Grand Avenue, southeast of West Northside Drive. The grave is in Block 101, Lot 14, Space 1.

- God-fearing assassins are few in the annals of the Old West, but James Brown Miller (1861–1909) was one. His church-going habits earned him the nickname "Deacon Jim," while his hired gun earned him another, "Killer Miller." After murdering his own brother-in-law at the age of twenty-three, Miller began a cold-blooded rampage across the Southwest. In 1894 he killed Sheriff Bud Frazer in Pecos, Texas (see

"Ranger" George Frazer's Grave, Fort Stockton, chapter 5), and continued to kill men for fun and profit, specializing in assassinating lawmen. He was even hired to kill legendary sheriff Pat Garrett, but most experts agree that Garrett was killed by someone else.

Miller was known for wearing a long, black coat, which concealed a steel, bullet-proof breastplate—a bit of fashion that inspired the costume worn by Clint Eastwood in 1964's *Fistful of Dollars*.

Miller had dodged serious jail time throughout his bloody career, but in 1909 he accepted $1,700 to ambush an ex-marshal in Ada, Oklahoma. After the killing, Miller was arrested by a Texas Ranger and extradited to Oklahoma, where impatient locals couldn't wait for a trial. Miller and three cohorts were dragged from jail to an old barn to be lynched. "Let the record show," Miller proudly announced, "that I've killed fifty-one men." He asked that his diamond ring be given to his wife and that he be allowed to die wearing his trademark black hat and frock. "I'd like to have my coat," he said. "I don't want to die naked."

The mob let him wear the hat, but not the coat, as he was strung up. The four dead prisoners hung from the barn rafters for four hours, until a photographer could record the lynching for posterity. For years, pictures of the lynched men were sold as postcards in Ada. His wife—a cousin of John Wesley Hardin—got the ring and buried him in Fort Worth (GPS: 32.76799 / -97.34829).

• If the name Luke Short sounds familiar, maybe you're thinking of the pseudonymous western writer whose pulpy novels were published from 1935 to 1976. But the real Luke Short (1854–1893) was a gunfighter and gambler friend of the Earps, Doc Holliday, and Bat Masterson. After scrapes in Tombstone and Dodge City, Short came to Fort Worth, where he had a stake in the White Elephant Saloon (106 East Exchange Avenue, or GPS 32.788767 / -97.348807). Problem is, ex-marshal Jim "Longhair" Courtright (1848–1887) was running a protection racket, and Short refused to pay. In classic fashion, they stood face to face on a Fort Worth street and drew. Short's first shot clipped off Courtright's right thumb, rendering his double-action revolver useless. Before Courtright could switch hands, Short shot him three more times in one of the most famous Old West gunfights. In fact, it's reenacted every February 8 in front of the bar, which is across the street from the equally historic Stockyards Hotel (where maybe Bonnie and Clyde spent a night).

Short died of congestive heart failure six years later and was buried in Oakwood (GPS: 32.77087 / -97.34821)—not far from Courtright (GPS: 32.76955 / -97.34908).

- For more than a hundred years, the grave of madam Mary Porter (1844–1905) in Oakwood's "soiled doves' row" lay unmarked (GPS: 32.76881 / -97.34916). Although she was Fort Worth's most famous brothel-keeper (no relation to San Antonio madam Fannie Porter), she was buried without fanfare with three other prostitutes when she died at age sixty-one. In 2009 Fort Worth police sergeant Kevin Foster donated a stone and three local history buffs paid to engrave it with Porter's epitaph: "Call Me Madam."

- Millionaire racehorse owner James Madison Brown (1839–1892) played both sides of the crime game. As sheriff of Lee County, he presided over the hanging of gunslinger Wild Bill Longley . . . but in 1892 he was gunned down by Chicago police who were attempting to arrest him for one of about fourteen murders he committed while sheriff. (GPS: 32.77087 / -97.34789)

WILD BUNCH PHOTO STUDIO
Fort Worth

John Swartz's studio was formerly at 705½ Main Street in Fort Worth. The old building is long gone and is now an office building. GPS: 32.753164 / -97.330142

After a September 1900 bank robbery in Winnemucca, Nevada, Butch Cassidy's Hole in the Wall Gang split up and met in Fort Worth. Feeling cocky, the gang's five main outlaws—Butch, Sundance Kid,

The Wild Bunch sat for a portrait that became one of the Old West's most famous images. JOHN SCHWARTZ

Harvey Logan, Ben Kilpatrick, and Will Carver—dressed up in city duds and posed for a group photo at John Swartz's studio. Swartz was so delighted by the soon-to-be-famous image that he posted a print in his downstairs window, where it was spotted by a passing Wells Fargo agent who recognized Harvey Logan. The gang had unwittingly posed for its own wanted poster.

Swartz eventually left Texas and died in West Virginia. The rough-and-tumble district near the studio known as Hell's Half Acre was eventually redeveloped and renamed Sundance Square after the famous outlaw.

Also see "Grave of Outlaws Ben Kilpatrick and Ole Hobek" (Sanderson) and "Outlaw Will Carver's Grave" (Sonora), both in chapter 5.

KILLER OLIN STEVENS'S HOUSE
Fort Worth

The house is at 1408 Morrison Drive, in the southwestern block of Morrison and I-30. This is private property. GPS: 32.758089 / -97.190983

In 1933 Olin D. Stevens (1894–1972) and four other criminals robbed a mail truck of $72,000. But rather than share the money, the stingy Stevens killed three of his cohorts and dumped their bodies off the north side of the East First Street Bridge (GPS: 32.766166 / -97.270492) into the Trinity River. Stevens was convicted of the robbery and the murders and imprisoned at Alcatraz and Leavenworth. He died at age seventy-eight after his release and is buried in Hot Springs, Arkansas.

The murder likely happened here at what used to be Stevens's home (now a day-care center) in a room under the stairway. Secret passages were found under the house, and most were subsequently filled in. The stolen money was never located, and for years the neighborhood kids fantasized that it was still hidden somewhere in the house.

GRAVE OF PRO FOOTBALLER DARRENT WILLIAMS
Fort Worth

Laurel Land–Fort Worth Cemetery is at 7100 Crowley Road. The grave is on the western edge of the small Christ Circle just south of the main office. GPS: 32.64240 / -97.34941

Denver Broncos' cornerback Darrent Williams (1982–2007) was a rising star, only twenty-four, when his stretch limo was sprayed with bullets after a nightclub dispute on New Year's Eve in Denver. More than twenty bullets hit the limo, but only one hit Williams in the neck, killing him. A Crips gang-banger was charged with Williams's first-degree murder after he allegedly confessed to the crime in a jailhouse letter.

RANGER TOM HICKMAN'S GRAVE
Gainesville

Fairview Cemetery is 5 blocks east of FM 372, on the east side of Fair Avenue. The grave is in the southwest corner of Section 4. GPS: 33.63071 / -97.12634

Once a performer in the famous Miller Brothers' 101 Ranch Show, Thomas Hickman (1886–1962) was a deputy sheriff in his native Cooke County when he became a Texas Ranger in 1919, just as the state was about to explode with crime. During Prohibition and the Great Depression, Hickman kept the peace—or tried—in the rough and rowdy oil boomtowns of North Texas. And during the gangster days when bank robbers were knocking off an average of one Texas bank every day, Hickman chased many of them, including the notorious Santa Claus bank robbers in Cisco. But Hickman never gave up on the cowboy life: In 1924 he judged the first American rodeo in England, and in 1926 he judged Madison Square Garden's first-ever rodeo.

Also see "Santa Claus Bank Robbery" (Cisco).

Home of Jesse James and John Wilkes Booth . . . Maybe

The two most famous residents of the little town of Granbury might never have actually lived there . . . or maybe they did. It's a little confusing, but it illustrates how the American cult of celebrity—especially a morbid fascination with the possibility that celebrities occasionally fake their deaths—goes way back before Elvis.

It all began in 1870, five years after the Lincoln assassination, when a young man named John St. Helen settled in nearby Glen Rose, Texas, where he took a job as a bartender and acted in the local theater. He reportedly had an encyclopedic knowledge of Shakespeare and a remarkable stage presence. But when the daughter of a local politician invited a slew of U.S. Army officers and a federal marshal to her fabulous wedding, St. Helen mysteriously disappeared.

In 1871 he popped up in Granbury, just up the road. He again worked as a bartender at a local saloon (now a bakery at 137 Pearl Street, or GPS 32.44211 / -97.78662) and befriended a local lawyer named Finis Bates (future grandfather of actress Kathy Bates). Bates noted years later that although St. Helen was a teetotaler, he drank himself silly on one day of every year, April 14—the anniversary of Lincoln's shooting.

While in Granbury, St. Helen got sick and believed he would soon die. Secretly, he whispered to his friend Bates, "My name is not John St. Helen. I am John Wilkes Booth, assassin of Abraham Lincoln." To be sure, he bore a resemblance to the famed actor and dastardly killer. His age (around forty) was about right, and his theatrical demeanor gave one pause. Plus, he told a remarkable story of mistaken identity on the Virginia farm where Booth was supposedly killed by federal troops.

But St. Helen didn't die. He recovered long enough to disappear again, reportedly leaving behind a pistol wrapped in a Washington newspaper dated April 15, 1865.

That was the last anyone heard of St. Helen—until 1903, when an itinerant housepainter named David George committed suicide in Enid, Oklahoma. He, too, had confessed his "true identity" to a local widow, who described him as an intelligent man who often quoted Shakespeare when soused. And, the coroner discovered George's right leg had been broken just above the ankle years before, and he was born in the same year as Booth. They wondered, might David George's alias be a combination of two Lincoln conspirators' names, David Herold

Did John Wilkes Booth survive the manhunt after Lincoln's assassination?

and George Atzerodt, both hanged for their roles in the assassination plot?

George/St. Helen/Booth's corpse was mummified and displayed for two years in the front window of an Enid funeral home until Finis Bates came to identify George as his old friend, John St. Helen. He claimed the body, had it positively identified by Booth relatives, then sent it on a carnival sideshow tour as the mummy of John Wilkes Booth.

In 1931 a team of doctors and detectives X-rayed the mummy. They allegedly found a broken leg and thumb, and a scar on the neck that matched wounds Booth was known to have suffered. Oddly, they also found a corroded signet ring in the mummy's stomach—bearing the initial *B*. Suddenly, people began to wonder . . . could it be?

In 1937 the mummy reportedly attracted more than $100,000 from sideshow gawkers. Various carnivals displayed the mummy over the years until it vanished completely in 1973.

But Booth wasn't the last outlaw to come back from the dead in Granbury.

In 1947 a one-hundred-year-old man named J. Frank Dalton from Lawton, Oklahoma, claimed he was the real Jesse James. Now, most folks believe James was assassinated by Robert Ford to collect a big reward, but Dalton spun a tale of how he and Bob Ford had faked his 1882 death and a lookalike was buried in his place. Like David George, his name even hinted at a connection: The *J.* might have stood for Jesse, and Frank was Jesse's infamous brother's name.

Near the end of his life, Dalton moved to Granbury, where a friend would sometimes charge gawkers

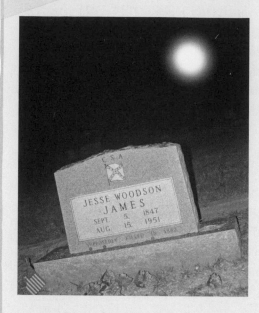

J. Frank Dalton was one hundred years old when he first revealed that he was, in fact, Jesse James. Was he?

a quarter to see the real Jesse James on his deathbed. Many were convinced. When he died in 1951 at 104, the coroner found thirty-two bullet scars, rope damage on his neck, and burn scars on his feet—all matching wounds Jesse James suffered. After the former sheriff positively identified Dalton's corpse as James, his official death certificate was issued in the name of Jesse Woodson James.

In 1995 forensic anthropologists determined that DNA from the corpse in Jesse James's grave in Kearney, Missouri, matched James family descendants. But skeptics persisted, and in 2000 Dalton's body was exhumed, too. Unfortunately, the wrong body was exhumed, and no further attempts were made.

Dalton/James's Granbury headstone (still over the wrong man) remains boldly engraved: "Jesse

Woodson James . . . supposedly killed in 1882." The grave is well marked in Granbury Cemetery (GPS: 32.45272 / -97.78477).

Today, almost no serious James scholar believes Dalton was the outlaw, although some believe he might have once ridden with the James Gang. But don't start an argle-bargle with the folks in Granbury, who enjoy a modest tourism boon thanks to the erstwhile Booth and James characters. On the wall at the former Pearl Street saloon (now a bakery), where "Booth" worked, is a mural depicting the two shooting a bear.

Oh, but we're not quite done with Texas's "Outlaw Relocation Program." Read on!

GRAVE OF OLLIE ROBERTS (AKA BILLY THE KID)
Hamilton

Oakwood Cemetery is on the east side of US 281 just north of Hamilton. GPS: 31.71685 / -98.11908

Maybe you've been to the "official" grave of William "Billy the Kid" Bonney in Fort Sumner, New Mexico, but you must come to Hamilton, Texas, to visit the grave of Ollie "Brushy Bill" Roberts (1858–1950), who claimed in his twilight years to be the genuine Billy the Kid. At least six books have been written about him, and lots of people are convinced Brushy Bill is the real Kid.

When Brushy Bill's "true" identity was discovered in 1948, he claimed a look-alike friend was actually killed by Sheriff Pat Garrett and that he then embarked on an incredibly adventurous life as a Wild West show performer, a Pinkerton agent, an aide to "Hanging Judge" Isaac Parker, a Rough Rider, and a volunteer with Pancho

Was Ollie Roberts really Billy the Kid?

Villa. In 1949 he attended a birthday party for his friend J. Frank Dalton, who claimed to be the real Jesse James. In 1950 Brushy Bill asked the New Mexico governor for a pardon, but his case was never heard. He died of a heart attack on a Hamilton street at age ninety.

Unconvinced? Brushy Bill has *two* museums dedicated to his life. Visit the Billy the Kid Memorial Museum at 211-C North Rice Street in Hamilton (GPS: 31.70523 / -98.12366; 254-386-3641).Owner Myrna Carpenter actually knew Brushy Bill, and among the period pieces she displays are a pair of his spurs and a leather holster. You may also visit the Billy the Kid Museum at 114 North Pecan Street, Hico (GPS: 31.98192 / -98.03087; 254-796-4004; www.billythekidmuseum.com).

Also see "Site of Sheriff Pat Garrett's Former Home" (Uvalde, chapter 1) and "Home of Jesse James and John Wilkes Booth . . . Maybe" (Granbury).

Murder of "Diamond Bessie"

Every century has its trial, and one of the nineteenth century's biggest was the murder case against Abe Rothschild, a swindling scion of an old-money Ohio family, for the murder of his lover (some say wife) Annie Stone Moore, a dancer and prostitute better known as "Diamond Bessie."

On January 19, 1877, Abe and a bejeweled Bessie registered as husband and wife at the Brooks House hotel in Jefferson (now a historic vacant lot at GPS 32.75742 / -94.34636). For the next couple of days, they wandered around the bustling river port city, arguing loudly. On January 21, Abe and Bessie crossed the bridge into the Big Cypress Bayou—but Abe came back alone and quickly left town. A passerby found Bessie's corpse a couple of weeks later, shot in the head and stripped of its jewelry.

Texas sent Sheriff Johnny Vines to Ohio to arrest Rothschild and bring him back for the first major murder trial in Texas history. He shared a cell with a railroader named Jim Currie (1840–1899), who was accused of shooting two actors, killing one and wounding the second, a man named Maurice Barrymore, patriarch of the acting Barrymore family and Drew's great-grandfather. Currie was eventually acquitted.

Represented by future congressman David Culberson (1830–1900) and former Confederate general Hinchie Mabry (1829–1884), Rothschild was convicted, but the verdict was overturned on appeal. He was acquitted in his second trial, but the experience didn't stop his criminal behavior: In 1902 he was convicted of swindling diamond dealers in Pennsylvania. Nonetheless, the murder case remains officially unsolved and is still studied by lawyers and investigators.

After the murder, citizens collected $150 to bury Bessie in an unmarked grave in Oakwood Cemetery on North Alley Street, about 5 blocks north of Broadway/ TX 49 (her grave is at GPS 32.76618 / -94.34745), while rumors swirled that she had been pregnant. In the 1890s a distinguished outsider with a patch over his eye knelt at the grave and paid the caretaker to take special care of the spot. In the 1930s a local donor paid for a headstone, and in the 1940s the local garden club erected a wrought-iron fence around the grave.

Other key players in the Diamond Bessie murder case are buried nearby. Sheriff Vines (GPS: 32.76705 / -94.34825) and lawyers Culberson (GPS: 32.76733 / -94.34777) and Mabry (GPS: 32.76672 / -94.34797) are all in the historic section just north of Bessie's grave.

The Excelsior Hotel (211 West Austin Street, or GPS 32.75585 / -94.34560) displays some fascinating artifacts related to the famous case, including a photo of Abe in his jail cell, a register signed by Abe Rothschild, and the original guest book entry for the jury.

But Diamond Bessie's memory isn't dead. Every spring, Abe's trial is reenacted for the town's Pilgrimage Days.

OAKWOOD CEMETERY
Jefferson

Oakwood Cemetery is on North Alley Street, about 5 blocks north of Broadway/TX 49.

- Although a Confederate marker graces outlaw Cullen Baker's grave, he was a deserter and a slacker who kept killing freed slaves, Reconstructionists (better known in Texas as "carpetbaggers"), and Union sympathizers long after the war ended. Baker (1835–1869) was nineteen when he killed his first man, and by the time he was thirty, the *New York Tribune* had nicknamed him the "Swamp Fox of the Sulphur." His reputation as a quick-draw gunslinger was a myth, and he was actually a vengeful alcoholic killer, but his bloody one-man rampage for defeated Southern "values" earned him a certain prestige. The most reliable account of his death at age thirty-four claims that Baker drank whiskey his own father-in-law had laced with strychnine. His body was then shot several times, delivered to a U.S. Army outpost near Jefferson, and displayed publicly before being buried (GPS: 32.76653 / -94.34808). A hundred years later, western author Louis L'Amour wrote about Baker in his novel *The First Fast Draw*.

- In the 1800s two feuding outlaws named Robertson and Rose (their first names were never recorded) killed each other in a gunfight. The local sheriff was so annoyed by their long-simmering bad blood that he ordered their corpses to be buried side-by-side, and their graves (GPS: 32.76698 / -94.34815) to be literally chained together for eternity— which they are.

When two feuding patriarchs killed each other in a brawl, the
local sheriff was creative in dispensing postmortem justice.

KAREN SILKWOOD'S GRAVE
Kilgore

Danville Cemetery is on the north side of Old Longview Road
just east of US 259. GPS: 32.40235 / -94.82983

Karen Silkwood (1946–1974) was a lab technician at Kerr-
McGee's Cimarron River Plutonium Plant in Crescent, Oklahoma,
when she reportedly discovered some dangerous radioactive spills
and missing plutonium. But plant managers didn't seem worried
by her reports, so she began agitating for reforms. Contaminated
by plutonium found in her apartment, she joined a strike by atomic
workers at the plant.

Silkwood left a union meeting on November 13, 1974, to meet
with an Atomic Energy Commission official and a *New York Times*

reporter, but she never arrived: She died in a one-car crash with extraordinary levels of sleep drugs in her body. Many people believe foul play was involved, but no charges were ever filed. Meryl Streep starred in the 1984 film *Silkwood* about the case. Silkwood was buried in Kilgore, her hometown.

Local legend maintains that Silkwood's grave glows with a greenish mist at night.

KFC MASS MURDER
Kilgore

The former KFC building is now an ophthalmology clinic at 800 US 259 North. GPS: 32.387883 / -94.866992

Just after closing on September 23, 1983, armed robbers held up this small-town Kentucky Fried Chicken restaurant, taking $2,000 from the cash register and valuables from five people inside. But rather than just take the money and run, the robbers abducted the five—Opie Ann Hughes, 38; David Maxwell, 20; Joseph Johnson, 20; Monty Landers, 19; and Mary Tyler, 37—and forced them to lie down side-by-side beside a dark, rural oilfield road. All were shot at least twice, execution-style, in the back of the head; Hughes's corpse was found 50 yards away from the others, raped.

The mass murder went unsolved for twenty-five years until DNA tests not available in 1983 linked career criminal Darnell Hartsfield and his cousin Romeo Pinkerton to the killings. The two pleaded guilty to the murders and are each serving five consecutive life terms. A suspected third killer has never been identified.

LUBY'S CAFETERIA MASSACRE SITE
Killeen

The building is at 1705 East Central Texas Expressway. GPS: 31.09352 / -97.72392

Around lunchtime on October 16, 1991, a deranged ex-seaman named George Hennard crashed his Ford Ranger through the front window of a Luby's Cafeteria and into the crowded dining room. He got out of his truck with two semiautomatic handguns and methodically began executing the stunned diners.

Over the next twelve minutes, he killed twenty-three people and wounded twenty more before police arrived. During the ensuing shootout with cops, Hennard shot himself. It was the deadliest American shooting spree until the 2007 Virginia Tech massacre. Though no motive was ever established for the mass murder, evidence emerged later that Hennard was a paranoid who believed white women had formed a cartel to prevent him from dating and getting a job. Fifteen of his twenty-three victims were women.

Luby's remodeled and reopened the cafeteria five weeks after the massacre but ultimately closed the restaurant for good in 2000. A Chinese buffet has occupied the building ever since. Hennard crashed through the window just to the right of the main entrance.

A memorial to the twenty-three victims was erected in Community Center Park on East Veterans Memorial Boulevard (GPS: 31.10889 / -97.71232), about a mile north of the restaurant site. The mansion where Hennard lived at the time is at 301 East 14th Avenue, in nearby Belton (GPS: 31.068405 / -97.455592).

No memorial to killer George Jo Hennard exists. In fact, an orchestrated effort has been made to erase his memory entirely. His corpse was cremated and his ashes scattered at sea. The Killeen Police Department later destroyed his guns and battering-ram pickup to expunge the memory.

Also see the Al and Ursula Gratia listing in "Fort Sam Houston National Cemetery" (San Antonio, chapter 1) and "Mass-Murderer George Hennard's House" (Belton).

HORRELL-HIGGINS FEUD PLAQUE
Lampasas

The plaque is on the west side of the courthouse lawn along South Live Oak Street. GPS: 31.06544 / -98.17799

Family feuds were often violent. In 1873 the five troublemaking Horrell boys killed several state policemen in Lampasas but escaped justice by fleeing to New Mexico. There they stirred up more trouble, and seventeen men were killed on both sides. Settling back in Lampasas, they ran afoul of the Higgins family, and a bloody feud began. It only ended in 1878 when all but one Horrell brother were dead—two lynched by vigilantes in Lampasas—and the families agreed to settle their animosities without further bloodshed.

DALTON GANG'S LAST RAID
Longview

The First National Bank once stood at 200 North Fredonia Street. GPS: 32.494813 / -94.738846

In 1894 the infamous Dalton Gang—led by Bill Dalton—robbed the First National Bank of $2,000 in coins, bills, and bank notes. But their escape was foiled, and a bloody gunfight killed two civilians and outlaw Jim Wallace (now buried in Longview's Greenwood Cemetery). The gang scattered, but two weeks later, after Bill Dalton tried to use some of the bank's money to buy supplies in Ardmore, Oklahoma, he was shot dead while resisting arrest.

BLACK WIDOW BETTY LOU BEETS'S DEATH HOUSE
Mabank

Beets's former mobile home sat at about 128 Red Bluff Loop, a now-vacant, overgrown lot directly across from the intersection of Lake Arrowhead Drive and Red Bluff Loop, on an inlet to

**Clear Creek Reservoir about 4 miles south of Mabank in Chero-
kee Shores. GPS: 32.256487 / -96.096007**

Ex-stripper and "black widow" Betty Lou Beets died by lethal
injection in 2000, only the second woman executed in Texas since it
reinstated the death penalty in 1976. In 1983 she shot her fifth husband, a firefighter, while he slept to collect his $100,000 life insur-
ance and buried him under a decorative wishing well in her front
yard. When cops dug up the body two years later, they also found
the murdered corpse of Betty Lou's long-missing fourth husband
buried out back.

At the trial it came out that Betty Lou had also shot and
wounded her second husband and ran over her third with a car,
but both survived. During her appeals, a judge described the
granny Betty Lou as "a greedy and insensitive killer, the kind of
succubus who has managed to capture the romantic imagination
of Americans in such modern cinematic classics as *Body Heat* and
Black Widow."

The crime was detailed in *Buried Memories* by Irene Pence (Pinnacle, 2001).

TEXAS CADET MURDER
Mansfield

**The Serenity Gardens Memorial is in Julian Field Park at 1531
East Broad Street. GPS: 32.566786 / -97.122499**

Sixteen-year-old Adrianne Jones (1979–1995) was beaten and
shot to death by her one-time high school lover, David Graham,
and his jealous teen girlfriend, Diane Zamora. A few months after
the cruel killing, Graham entered the U.S. Air Force Academy and
Zamora entered the U.S. Naval Academy, where she bragged about
the murder to her roommates. Eventually, Graham and Zamora
were both convicted in highly publicized trials; Graham was given
sixty years in prison and Zamora got life without parole. In 2003

Zamora—who spends twenty-three hours a day in her cell—married another inmate (ironically, not Graham) by proxy.

Jones's body was cremated, but in 2001 the City of Mansfield dedicated Serenity Gardens in her memory. The case inspired a 1997 TV movie, *Love's Deadly Triangle: The Texas Cadet Murder,* and the 1998 book *Blind Love.*

OUTLAW JIM REED'S GRAVE
McKinney

Settlers Field is part of Pecan Grove Cemetery at the intersection of TX 5 and Eldorado Parkway, south of the downtown area. Reed's unmarked grave lies somewhere in the paupers' section. GPS: 33.179496 / -96.615787

The first husband of "bandit queen" Belle Starr, Jim Reed (1845–1874) rode with Quantrill's Raiders during the Civil War, then later joined the James-Younger gang. He married Belle in Scyene, Texas, in 1866 but moved his family to California and Oklahoma to avoid capture after a string of robberies and murders. The law finally caught up to Reed in 1874 when he was shot in Paris, Texas, by Deputy John Morris, a distant cousin who didn't collect the $4,000 bounty on his head.

Belle (1848–1889) lived a life of crime, romancing various Younger brothers before she married Indian bandit Sam Starr in 1880. She was shotgunned in the back on a country road near her cabin in Eufala, Oklahoma, just two days before her forty-first birthday. No suspects were ever arrested.

COLLIN COUNTY PRISON
McKinney

The prison is at 115 Kentucky Street, just off the downtown McKinney Square. GPS: 33.19666 / -96.61586

In the late 1800s the citizens of Collin County apparently weren't satisfied with a mere county jail. They wanted a prison. Designed by famed Austin architect F. E. Ruffini—who would later design the University of Texas's Old Main Building—the fortress-like prison of white ashlar limestone in the High Victorian Italianate style opened its doors in 1880. After ninety-nine years as a jail, the old building was renovated and has recently housed many different businesses.

Prison "guests" have included outlaw Frank James and Manson henchman Charles "Tex" Watson, who participated in the 1969 Helter Skelter murders of actress Sharon Tate and six others. Another notable prisoner was killer Ray "Elzie" Hamilton of the Barrow Gang, who hacksawed his way out of the Collin County Prison in 1932. He was later captured and executed in Huntsville's "Old Sparky" electric chair in 1935, but to this day, one of the iron bars in the second-story window where Hamilton escaped remains halfway sawed.

Also see "Gang Member Ray Hamilton's Grave" (Bonnie and Clyde chapter) and "'Tex' Watson's Childhood Home" (Copeville).

Springtime for the Black Sox

In March 1919 the Chicago White Sox gathered for spring training, as they had for the past three seasons, in Mineral Wells, Texas. Stars like "Shoeless Joe" Jackson, Eddie Collins, Eddie Cicotte, and Lefty Williams were all there, just two seasons after they'd won the World Series. Owner Charlie Comiskey believed the town's therapeutic waters and spas would be good for his players, already expected to go to the 1919 World Series.

But the star-filled White Sox proved to be star-crossed. They went to the World Series as prohibitive favorites against the weaker Cincinnati Reds, but seven players—Jackson, Cicotte, Williams, Chick Gandil, Swede Risberg, Hap Felsch, and Fred McMullin—conspired with big-time gamblers to lose the Series (an eighth player, Buck Weaver, knew about the fix but didn't participate). They were promised $100,000, but most of the money was never paid. In 1920 the eight "Black Sox" were acquitted in a criminal trial but were banned from baseball for life by Commissioner Kennesaw Mountain Landis after the biggest sports scandal in American history.

The White Sox never went back to Mineral Wells; the team moved its spring training to Waco in 1920, Waxahachie in 1921, and Seguin in 1922–23. The old

Shoeless Joe Jackson (left) poses with two White Sox teammates at their Mineral Wells spring-training field in 1919.

spring-training ballpark where Shoeless Joe and his Sox played is now a business strip on the southeast corner of SE 14th Avenue and East Hubbard Street/US 180 (GPS: 32.808746 / -98.099461).

One site still stands . . . sort of. That fateful spring, the team stayed at Mineral Wells's plush new Crazy Water Hotel (GPS: 32.811772 / -98.113103), a historic 1914 hotel that burned in 1924 and was rebuilt on the same site. It's now a retirement community.

ASSASSIN MALCOLM WALLACE'S GRAVE
Mount Pleasant
Nevill's Chapel Baptist Church Cemetery is at 113 CR 3210. GPS: 33.19474 / -94.95634

A former marine and University of Texas student body president, Malcolm "Mac" Wallace (1921–1971) came to be known as Lyndon Baines Johnson's hatchet man. It started when he was involved in a love triangle with LBJ's sister in 1951. When her other lover blackmailed her, Wallace killed him. But while his jury favored the death penalty, the judge only wrist-slapped Wallace with a suspended five-year prison sentence. Years later, LBJ confidant and financier Billie Sol Estes claimed Wallace killed eight people on LBJ's orders—including President John F. Kennedy. Some conspiracy theorists suggest he recruited Lee Harvey Oswald and Jack Ruby for the JFK assassination, and they place Wallace in the Texas School Book Depository and on the "grassy knoll" on November 22, 1963.

Wallace died in 1971 when his car crashed into a bridge abutment 3.5 miles south of Pittsburg, Texas (GPS: 32.92733 / -94.95898). He was forty-nine.

The Lynching of Henry Smith

One of Texas's most horrifying examples of vigilante cruelty—the 1893 lynching of accused child rapist and murderer Henry Smith, a mildly retarded black man, in the small town of Paris—was so ghastly that it sparked a debate across the South about mob violence, especially against blacks. Some have even surmised that without the political, moral, and social friction that followed Smith's lynching, the American civil rights movement sixty years later might have been delayed or quashed altogether.

It all began when Myrtle Vance, the three-year-old daughter of a local deputy, was found dead on February 1, 1893. Since Smith (1870–1893) had allegedly threatened revenge on the girl's father after a beating and was likely the last person to see Myrtle alive, suspicion turned to the slow-witted handyman.

Three-year-old Myrtle Vance's murder set in motion one of the most shocking lynchings in American history.

When Smith heard a mob was forming, he fled to Arkansas, but he was captured and returned by train to Paris, which was now teeming with 10,000 angry citizens bent on revenge. His captors claim Smith confessed to the crime during the trip. At the Texas & Pacific Railroad depot in Paris (GPS: 33.65035 / -95.55591), Smith was seated on a carnival float and paraded through town to a wooden scaffold built in the prairie about 300 yards from the depot.

There, Smith was stripped naked and tied to a stake while the infuriated throng—including children—watched and cheered. A newspaper reporter recounted the lynching in terrifying detail:

> A tinner's furnace was brought on filled with irons heated white. Taking one, [Henry Vance, the victim's father] thrust it under one and then the other side of his victim's feet, who, helpless, writhed as the flesh scarred and peeled from the bones. . . . when the iron was pressed to [Smith's] most tender part he broke silence for the first time and a prolonged scream of agony rent the air. . . . By turns Smith screamed, prayed, begged and cursed his torturer. . . . His tongue was silenced by fire, and thenceforth he only moaned or gave a cry that echoed over the prairie like the wail of a wild animal. Then his eyes were put out. . . . Smith and the clothing about his lower limbs were then saturated with oil as was the platform. . . . Slowly the flames wrapped him in their bluish veil. . . . The head slowly raised and a broken, quivering cry broke the breathless silence . . . then

the cords binding the arms burned and he raised the crisped and blackened stumps to wipe the sightless sockets of his eyes. . . . Then he toppled forward upon the platform and laid there writhing and quivering in the greedy flames.

But Henry Smith was not yet dead. He rose on the stumps of his charred feet and tumbled off the scaffold, where onlookers heaped burning timbers on top of him as he crawled blindly across the dirt. When he was finally declared dead, his executioners raked his bones from the coals, and the crowd took them as souvenirs.

The actual spot of the lynching has been lost, although large vacant areas dot the general area where it happened (GPS: 33.64729 / -95.55598). Henry Smith's ashes are gone with the wind; whatever parts of him remained after souvenir hunters grabbed their macabre booty were left where they lay.

Later, Myrtle's family published a small book containing several photos taken of Smith's lynching, attempting to defend their behavior and make some money. A copy exists in the Paris Junior College archives (2400 Clarksville Street, or GPS 33.650167 / -95.529771).

Little Myrtle Vance was buried beneath an angelic headstone in Evergreen Cemetery (Block 4, or GPS 33.64206 / -95.55251) in a family plot. To this day, some debate whether Henry Smith really killed her, but one thing is absolutely certain: Nobody was ever prosecuted for his lynching.

GRAVE OF BUSHWHACKER WILLIAM MARCHBANKS
Paris

Evergreen Cemetery is at 560 Evergreen Street, just off TX 24, less than a mile south of the Paris town square. The grave is in Block H. GPS: 33.64334 / -95.55091

Confederate guerrilla Captain Bill Marchbanks (1833–1912) had a reputation of being even crueler than his bushwhacking commander, William Quantrill, during the Civil War. This former lawman and son of a judge led several bloody raids in Kansas and Missouri and shared camps with the James and Younger brothers. His 1863 raid on Nevada, Missouri, led to the destruction of the town two days later. After the war he settled in Paris, Texas, where he eventually served as a town alderman—and one of its most respected citizens.

While you're in Evergreen Cemetery, be sure to visit Willet and Belinda Babcock's famous grave (GPS: 33.64307 / -95.55174), which is marked by an almost life-size statue of Jesus wearing cowboy boots.

You might also visit the grave of legendary cattle baron John Chisum (1824–1884), a close associate of both Billy the Kid and Sheriff Pat Garrett—and portrayed by John Wayne in the movies. He's also in Paris in the Chisum Family Cemetery at 1100 Washington Street (GPS: 33.653483 / -95.567267).

BOMBER BOBBY FRANK CHERRY'S GRAVE
Payne Springs

Payne Springs Cemetery is on the east side of TX 198, about 8 miles south of Mabank. The grave is in Block 17. GPS: 32.27789 / -96.07109

Ex-Klansman Bobby Frank Cherry (1930–2004) was one of four suspects in the killing of four black girls in the 1963 bombing of Birmingham's Sixteenth Street Baptist Church, one of the most shocking crimes of the civil rights era. But it took almost forty years to bring him to justice, during which time he moved to Mabank, Texas, where he worked as a clerk, a welder, and a cabbie while marrying several times and fathering fifteen children. In 2001 Cherry was the third and last person to be convicted in the bombing (a fourth suspect died before arrest); he died three years later of cancer in an Alabama prison. He was seventy-four.

The 2002 TV movie *Sins of the Father* was based on Cherry's role in the bombing.

RANGER BILL McDONALD'S GRAVE
Quanah

Historic Quanah Memorial Park is on FM 2640, off East Prairie Street on the northern edge of town. GPS: 34.30659 / -99.73000

Even though Captain Bill McDonald (1852–1918) patrolled some of the wildest parts of the Wild West, he's famous for using his brains more than his gun. His most renowned tactic was to extend a friendly hand to a suspect and then slap a pair of handcuffs on him in the flash of an eye.

McDonald is also credited with two quotes that summarize the Texas Rangers' mythic status: "No man in the wrong can stand up against a fellow that's in the right and keeps a comin'" and "One riot, one Ranger."

In 1896 McDonald was dispatched to Langtry to close down Judge Roy Bean's illegal Fitzsimmons-Maher prizefight. Legend says he was in the judge's Jersey Lilly Saloon before the fight when a patron was poised to throw something at a slow waiter. McDonald reportedly warned, "I wouldn't do that if I were you," and the angry patron retorted, "Do you wanna take it up?" McDonald rose from his chair and said, "I done took it up." The patron—Bat Masterson—apologized.

After his Ranger days, McDonald served as a bodyguard for presidents Teddy Roosevelt and Woodrow Wilson.

Also see "Judge Roy Bean's Grave" (Del Rio), "Judge Roy Bean's Jersey Lilly Saloon" (Langtry), and "Fitzsimmons-Maher Prizefight Site" (Langtry), all in chapter 5.

RANGER RED BURTON'S GRAVE
Riesel

Riesel Cemetery is on the west side of TX 6/North Memorial Street, about a mile north of town. The grave is in Section 2, which is the second block from the north end of the cemetery. GPS: 31.49132 / -96.93031

Marvin "Red" Burton (1885–1970) never really wanted to be a lawman, but he became one of Texas's best. The former Waco police chief was appointed a Ranger in 1922. Among his first cases was a series of axe murders and rapes, for which two men were ultimately convicted. But Burton had a hunch they weren't guilty, so he testified in their defense. When the real killer was eventually arrested in 1923, Burton helped control the crowd of 5,000 spectators who gathered to see Nathan Lee hang on the courthouse lawn in Angleton, Texas—the last legal hanging in Texas.

Burton is a member of the Texas Ranger Hall of Fame.

GRAVES OF VICTIMS DEVON AND DAMON ROUTIER
Rockwall

Rest Haven Memorial Park is at 2500 TX 66 East/Williams Street. The graves are in the Faith section, Lot 751, Spaces A/B. GPS: 32.93791 / -96.42370

Six-year-old Devon and five-year-old Damon were stabbed to death in their suburban Rowlett home one late summer night in 1996. Their mother, Darlie, also wounded, told police an intruder had attacked her and her sons with a butcher knife. But the deeper investigators delved into her story, the more they suspected Darlie herself. The high-living family was sinking into deep financial trouble. Worse, the materialistic, flashy Darlie had recently had another baby, suffered from postpartum depression, and contemplated suicide a month before the murders.

A few days after the boys' deaths, Darlie hosted a bizarre graveside party on what would have been Devon's seventh birthday, laughing, chewing bubble gum, and spraying Silly String—an odd celebration caught by a police camera. Darlie was arrested four days later and was eventually sentenced to die for Damon's murder. Many supporters still believe she did not commit the crime, however, and continue to agitate for a new trial.

THE PHANTOM KILLER OF TEXARKANA
Texarkana
The key crime scene (of several) is beside South Robinson Road, less than 1 mile south of US 67. GPS: 33.418493 / -94.08031

A grisly discovery was made on this spot in March 1946: the dead bodies of two teenagers, both shot in the back of the head with a .32-caliber pistol. Their corpses appeared to have been shot outside of their car, then put back inside. At the time, police didn't connect the killings to an attack a month earlier on two teenagers in a local lover's lane, but in April, when another teen couple was shot to death with a .32, police came to believe the cases were related and nicknamed their fiend the "Phantom Killer." At least five people were dead, and most of the women had been raped or molested, a fact usually omitted from 1940s newspapers.

In June a woman claimed that she had watched her husband, Youell Swinney, a career criminal and son of a Baptist preacher, kill his victims. Evidence mounted against Swinney, but some crucial police blunders doomed the murder case, so Swinney (1917–1994) was instead charged with car theft and went to prison for twenty-seven years. Released in 1974, he died in a Dallas nursing home in 1994. No further "Phantom Killer" murders occurred after his arrest, but the case remains officially open. (Perhaps a testament to human fear, some amateur sleuths have even suggested the Phantom Killer and the Zodiac Killer were the same man.)

The Phantom's dogged pursuer, Spanish-born Texas Ranger Manuel Gonzaullas (1891–1977), led a more adventurous life than most people dream about. Orphaned by the Galveston hurricane in 1900, he later joined the Mexican Army and was a U.S. Treasury agent before becoming a Texas Ranger in 1920. Nicknamed "Lone Wolf," he was one of the top Rangers during Texas's gangster period. In 1946 he investigated Texarkana's "Phantom Killer" murders, and was played by actor Ben Johnson in a 1977 B-movie about the case, *The Town That Dreaded Sundown*. After retiring in 1951, he became a Hollywood technical adviser. He died at age eighty-five in Dallas and was cremated. Gonzaullas is in the Texas Ranger Hall of Fame.

CULTIST DAVID KORESH'S GRAVE
Tyler

Tyler Memorial Park is at 12053 TX 64 West. The grave is in the Last Supper section. GPS: 32.35408 / -95.36824

Vernon Wayne Howell (1959–1993) was born to a fourteen-year-old unwed mother in Houston and largely raised by his grandparents. Dyslexic and odd, Howell dropped out of high school. At age twenty he joined his mother's church, the Seventh-Day Adventists, but was excommunicated after expressing an unhealthy interest in the pastor's young daughter.

After an unsuccessful stab at being a rock musician in California, he hooked up with the Branch Davidians, a splinter group of Seventh-Day Adventists that had settled near Waco, Texas, in 1955.

Howell began a love affair with the group's elderly prophetess, and soon a power struggle over the Branch Davidians' future leadership erupted. Howell was arrested for trying to kill his rival, his lover's son, but he was acquitted. (The rival had exhumed the corpse of an elderly follower and demanded that Howell bring her back to life to prove he was the Messiah. When cops failed to act on Howell's report about corpse abuse, he went back to the compound with guns and started shooting.)

Howell became the head of the Branch Davidians in 1990 when his rival was confined to a mental hospital after murdering another man who also claimed to be the Messiah. That's when Howell legally changed his name to "David Koresh" and settled with more than a hundred followers on the communal property east of Waco known as Mount Carmel. There he fathered at least fifteen children with various followers, took ownership of all the compound's women, and claimed to be Jesus in the flesh.

Branch Davidian leader David Koresh

In February 1993 federal agents tried to execute a warrant for Koresh as part of an investigation into allegations of illegal guns, drug-making, and child abuse at Mount Carmel. The ensuing shoot-out killed ten people, including four ATF agents, and started a fifty-one-day siege that ended when the entire compound burned during a federal assault on April 19, 1993. Koresh and seventy-nine followers were killed or committed suicide.

An examination of Koresh's badly charred corpse determined that he was killed by a gunshot wound to the forehead. Only four relatives—no clergy—attended his burial in an unmarked grave. The marker you see was placed long after the headlines had subsided.

On January 23, 2009, Koresh's mother, Bonnie Clark Haldeman (born 1944), was stabbed to death in Chandler, Texas, allegedly by her sister. She's buried beside her son and her husband, Roy.

Also see "Branch Davidian Compound" (Waco).

GRAVE OF MURDER VICTIM HOLLY MADDUX
Tyler
Cathedral in the Pines Cemetery is at 7825 South Broadway. The grave is in the Lake section, just north of the pond. GPS: 32.26369 / -95.30858

In the 1970s hippie guru Ira Einhorn called himself "The Unicorn" (because his German name translated as "one horn"). The burly, unkempt college professor hung out with counterculture figures like Allen Ginsberg and Abbie Hoffman, spewing New Age nonsense to lure naive young women to his bed.

One of them was Holly Maddux, a Texas girl who'd recently graduated from Bryn Mawr and moved into Einhorn's shabby Philadelphia apartment. But in 1977 Maddux had grown weary of her psychedelic lover. She told him she was moving out . . . and she disappeared. Then, in 1979, her mummified remains were found stuffed in a trunk in a closet in Einhorn's apartment. Her skull had been viciously bashed, but she was sealed alive in the trunk. When detectives told Einhorn what they discovered, he said only, "You found what you found."

Einhorn fled the United States in 1981 while awaiting trial; he was convicted in absentia in 1993 and sentenced to life in prison. Finally, in 2001, the fugitive Einhorn—free for almost twenty years—was extradited from France, reconvicted, and sentenced to life in a Pennsylvania prison.

The story was retold in the 1998 TV movie *Peace, Love, Murder: The Ira Einhorn Story* and Stephen Levy's 1988 book, *The Unicorn's Secret*.

BRANCH DAVIDIAN COMPOUND
Waco

Mount Carmel is northeast of Waco. Take FM 2491 (Elk Road) about 5 miles east of TX Loop 340. Bear left on FM 2491 when the road splits. In less than a half-mile, turn left on the gravel Double EE Ranch Road. The former Mount Carmel compound is about a quarter-mile on the right, beyond a green gate. This is private property. GPS: 31.595556 / -96.9875

For ten years a messianic cult leader named David Koresh preached his apocalyptic vision of the end times, prophesying Armageddon. So, in a way, Koresh proved right when, on April 19, 1993, Hell came to Waco.

Government agents believed the Branch Davidians' 77-acre Mount Carmel compound was rife with illegal guns, child sexual and physical abuse, drug manufacturing, and polygamy, and they attempted to execute a warrant. After a fifty-one-day siege at the compound, ATF and FBI agents assaulted the main building. A fire erupted—although whether the feds or the Davidians actually started it remains a mystery. In less than an hour, the entire structure burned to the ground.

Eighty Davidians died, including twenty-three children under seventeen. Some had committed suicide. In all, the seven-week siege and fatal inferno killed ninety people, including four ATF agents. It also sparked a wildfire of antigovernment insurgence, including the Oklahoma City bombing exactly two years later.

Today the site is little more than a healed-up scar on the spare Texas prairie. Although there has been talk of transforming the spot into a historic monument, it has not happened. But a few ghosts of the Branch Davidians remain.

The modest, one-room chapel you see was built roughly on the spot of Koresh's original chapel, which was part of the Davidians' larger living complex. The new Branch Davidian chapel is run by Charles Pace, who owns the property. A concrete swimming pool used by Koresh's 140 followers remains just behind the chapel. And a large live oak tree that often appeared in media interviews with Koresh before the siege is just inside the front gate to the right.

Because the sect believed doomsday was at hand, its members buried an old school bus as a bunker for food and ammunition just west of the swimming pool. Today fragments of the bus can still be seen protruding from the earth. Other underground bunkers and secret tunnels are said to exist, too.

Shortly after the tragedy, survivors planted a small grove of crape myrtle trees near the chapel with a memorial stone for each victim. Pace later moved most of the trees to the lane leading into the property, and the stones are now gathered in one spot on a different part of the property. Other haunting relics of the attack were left at the site for years after the compound's rubble was bulldozed—an old school bus, one of Koresh's motorcycles, and other odd bits and pieces—but they have all been removed. A small cemetery exists on the property, and some of the children who died in the fire are buried there.

During the siege federal agents occupied a small house across Double EE Ranch Road from the front gate (GPS: 31.59377 /

-96.990223); it was demolished in 2004. After the tragedy, memorials were erected here to the four ATF agents who were killed in the siege and to the victims of Timothy McVeigh's 1995 bombing of the Murrah building in Oklahoma City (which was inspired by the Waco disaster), but they are gone.

Many of the Waco victims—including several of the children Koresh fathered—were buried in paupers' graves at Restland Cemetery (intersection of South 12th and Martin Streets, or GPS 31.5327 / -97.1061). Koresh, whose real name was Vernon Howell, was buried in his hometown of Tyler, Texas; see "Cultist David Koresh's Grave."

TEXAS RANGER HALL OF FAME AND MUSEUM
Waco

The museum is off exit 335-B (University Parks Drive) on I-35. Hours are 9:00 a.m. to 4:30 p.m. daily, including weekends. Admission charged. GPS: 31.555463 / -97.118969

This official museum of the Texas Rangers features three main galleries chock-full of interesting artifacts from the history of the agency, which dates to 1823. The Homer Garrison Museum Gallery focuses on Ranger equipment through the years. The Brownfield Gallery houses case studies of important investigations such as kidnappings, riots, Bonnie and Clyde, and Texarkana's Phantom Killer. The Hall of Fame pays tribute to thirty-one distinguished and fallen Rangers. In addition, the Ranger Research Center offers researchers access to books, oral histories, archives, and photographs.

Among the items you'll see:

- A customized Colt .45 carried by Ranger Sergeant Andrew Carter, who arrested serial killer Rafael Resendez-Ramirez, known as the Railroad Killer.

- Guns found in Bonnie and Clyde's "death car" after they were ambushed by a Ranger-led posse in Louisiana. You can also see the guns used to kill the gangsters.

- A huge collections of guns, clothing, and other artifacts once used by some of the most famous Texas Rangers.

Want to look like a Ranger? In the museum store you can order an official, handmade Texas Rangers cowboy hat that meets the agency's strict specifications. Of course, for a little less, you can also buy a saddle-leather portfolio hand-tooled by prison inmates in the same shop where most Rangers have their gun belts made.

Travel tip: Don't confuse this official state institution with San Antonio's privately owned Texas Ranger museum (318 East Houston Street, or GPS 29.426366 / -98.488795). See "Texas Rangers and Buckhorn Museum" in chapter 1.

ASSASSINATED JOURNALIST
WILLIAM COWPER BRANN'S GRAVE
Waco

Oakwood Cemetery is at 2124 South Fifth Street. The grave is about 1.5 blocks west of the main entrance on the cemetery's Moore Street. GPS: 31.53807 / -97.11301

Newspaperman William Cowper Brann (1855–1898) was the son of a Presbyterian minister, but that didn't stop him from eviscerating people and institutions he viewed as especially sanctimonious hypocrites.

Following stints as an editor and reporter at several Texas papers, Braun revived a magazine called *The Iconoclast* in 1895. As its national circulation grew to almost 100,000, he heaped vitriol upon vituperation with a kind of harsh glee. He particularly loved skewering Baptists and Waco's Baylor University, a Baptist college he called "that great storm-center of misinformation." His scathing attacks inspired at least one fatal gunfight. Once, he was kidnapped by students who demanded a retraction of his comments; another time, a Baptist judge and two henchmen beat him up.

On April 1, 1898, Brann was shot in the back by an angry reader who loved Baylor University to death. Literally. With his dying energy, Brann was able to shoot and kill his assailant.

Brann was buried in Waco's venerable Oakwood Cemetery, and supporters erected an elaborate monument shaped like the lamp of truth. It bears only the initials *WCB* and a single word: *Truth*. The night it was erected, somebody fired two bullets into it, and the damage is still visible.

Childhood Homes of "Tex" Guinan

This much is known: Mary Louise Cecilia Guinan (1884–1933) was born a shopkeeper's daughter in Waco, Texas. After that, it becomes hard to separate the myth from the miss, and that's just the way she wanted it.

Guinan's Irish father ran a small market at Mary and Fourth Streets (it no longer exists at GPS 31.55589 / -97.12914). The family lived in two homes during their Waco years, one at 1436 Washington Avenue (razed for a small, modern building at GPS 31.54952 / -97.14178) and the other at 604 North Fourth Street (now a vacant lot except for the old front steps at GPS 31.56113 / -97.13532). She attended local church schools until her family moved to Denver when she was sixteen.

After a brief marriage ended in 1906, she pursued her dream of becoming a New York chorus girl and vaudevillian. In 1917 she starred in her first film, a silent called *The*

Wildcat—and the myth of "Tex" began to take root for America's first movie cowgirl. More films followed as the bawdy and beautiful Guinan became a popular attraction at some of New York's ritziest nightclubs.

At the start of Prohibition, the salty, Jazz Age diva opened the 300 Club (151 West 48th Street in Manhattan), where her guests and performers included mobsters, sports stars, famous (and future) actors, even evangelist Aimee Semple McPherson. Her illegal speakeasy was shut down many times but always reopened. In 1926 she reportedly earned more than $700,000 in ten months—and never spent more than nine hours in jail.

During her time Guinan popularized such phrases as "butter and egg men" (big-spending clubgoers) and "Never give a sucker an even break." She was known for greeting her customers at the door with a hearty "Hello, suckers!" Friend and rival Mae West even adopted some of Tex's wisecracking mannerisms and her bleached-blond hair. Al Capone often visited her clubs, and so did Rudolph Valentino.

The Crash of 1929 hit Tex hard. She made a few more movies (mostly playing thinly veiled versions of herself) and mounted an abortive European tour. While on tour with a new show in 1933, she contracted dysentery in Vancouver, British Columbia, and died at age forty-nine—one month before Prohibition ended. Among her dying wishes was to have an open-casket funeral "so the suckers can get a good look at me without a cover charge." More than 12,000 fans visited her body before she was buried at Calvary Cemetery in Queens, New York.

Lest anyone think this little Texas girl has been completely forgotten by history, it's worth noting that Whoopi Goldberg's extrasensory bartender on TV's *Star Trek: The Next Generation* was purposely named Guinan. *Texas Guinan: Queen of the Nightclubs* by Louise Berliner (University of Texas, 1993) is her most notable biography.

"DAHLIA" COP FINIS BROWN'S GRAVE
West

St. Mary's Catholic Cemetery is less than a mile south of the town on Old Cemetery Road. The grave is in Section 16, Row 3, near the back. GPS: 31.77397 / -97.08640

Described as an introspective bulldog, veteran homicide detective Finis A. Brown (1906–1990) was one of two lead detectives in the infamous 1947 "Black Dahlia" murder in Los Angeles. He was on the scene twelve minutes after the dismembered body was found. The case was never solved, but Brown reportedly was haunted by the grisly mystery long after he retired in 1964 and came to this small town in Texas. His headstone bears a replica of his gold badge and his photo.

Brown was portrayed by actor Ronny Cox in the 1975 TV movie *Who Is the Black Dahlia?*

RIVERSIDE CEMETERY
Wichita Falls

The cemetery is on the north side of TX 277, a quarter-mile west of I-44. It lies just east of the cemetery office at 204 Van Buren Street. GPS: 33.909704 / -98.50668

Bank Robbery of 1896

Justice might have been faster in the Old West, but for some people, it just wasn't fast enough.

On February 25, 1896, two ne'er-do-well cowboys named Foster Crawford and Elmer "Kid" Lewis robbed the City National Bank. When their ill-conceived plot spiraled out of control, they shot bank teller Frank Dorsey and escaped with $410. Lewis's horse was shot during the getaway, so he leapt on Crawford's with a posse in hot pursuit. That night, they were captured and jailed in Wichita Falls.

But an angry vigilante mob soon gathered. Battering down the jail's back door, they grabbed the robbers and took them to the bank they'd just robbed. A dastardly plan to burn them alive was set aside in favor of a hanging. Only twenty, Lewis taunted the furious crowd before the lynch mob hanged him from a telegraph pole on the corner in front of the bank. Crawford's last words were drunken gibberish, and his death throes at the end of the noose were so ugly that the sickened crowd dissipated. His death took ten long minutes—longer than the robbery.

Crawford's and Lewis's corpses dangled for a day before they were unceremoniously buried in the same grave under a tiny headstone in a lonely corner of Riverside Cemetery (Section Q, Lot 311, or GPS 33.91232 / -98.50748). One was placed in a coffin, and the other was put in the coffin's shipping crate. At least three generations of mothers descended from the wife of the local newspaper editor in 1896 have placed flowers at the grave annually for more than a hundred years. "She knew that they had a mother someplace," explained a granddaughter who continues the tradition today.

Bank teller Frank Dorsey, a beloved family man, was buried in a grand funeral. His impressive monument (GPS: 33.91203 / -98.50655) sits a scant few paces from the grave of Susan Parmer, outlaw Jesse James's sister.

Today only a remnant of the original bank building exists on the southeast corner of Seventh and Ohio Streets as a sandwich shop (GPS: 33.91420 / -98.49039), but the bank's original vault is part of the serving counter. The pole where Crawford and Lewis were lynched was removed in 1909, and a new street eventually covered the exact spot.

A rather bizarre artifact of the robbery can be seen a block away at the Museum of North Texas History (720 Indiana Avenue; www.month-ntx.org), where a jewelry box made from a hoof of Kid Lewis's dead horse is displayed.

Three notable graves at the historic Riverside Cemetery have direct ties to two of America's most infamous outlaws, Jesse and Frank James.

- The James boys' sister, Susan Lavenia James Parmer (1849–1889), lived near Wichita Falls with her husband, Allen, who rode with the marauding Quantrill's Raiders during the Civil War and joined the outlaw James Gang after the war. Jesse and Frank were frequent visitors at their home in nearby Archer City (GPS: 33.594805 / -98.625527). Susan died in childbirth at age forty and was buried under an ornate marble stone (Section N, Lot 221, or GPS 33.91215 / -98.50660). (A proven James Gang campsite can be found about a mile east of Decatur, Texas, at GPS: 33.231183 / -97.696417.)

- Allen Parmer (1848–1927), who was a Confederate bush-whacker at age fifteen, was wounded five times and consorted with the likes of Cole Younger and the James boys. He gave up the outlaw life and settled down to a variety of jobs after marrying the Jameses' sister. When she died, he remarried and moved to Alpine, Texas, but on a visit back to Wichita Falls at age seventy-nine, he died of a heart attack and was buried near his first wife (GPS: 33.91218 / -98.50661).

- Lee McMurtry (1840–1908) wasn't the first outlaw to become a sheriff, but he's among the few who actually became beloved, upstanding citizens. Like his friend Allen Parmer, McMurtry rode under the black flag of the vicious Quantrill's Raiders and later the James Gang, during which time the federal government posted a $10,000 bounty on his head. He left Missouri in 1871 to become a Texas cattle rancher. In 1896 he was elected Wichita County sheriff for four years, and he once enjoyed an emotional reunion with his war buddy (and ex-bandit) Cole Younger when the old outlaw brought his Wild West show to Wichita Falls. McMurtry died at age sixty-eight and was mourned as one of the city's most esteemed inhabitants. He was buried not far from Parmer (Section M, Lot 80, Space 3, or GPS 33.91215 / -98.50660).

4

JFK ASSASSINATION

On November 22, 1963, President John F. Kennedy was assassinated in Dallas, Texas.

That might be the only fact on which most of us agree (although a lunatic fringe still insists JFK is living on an island in the Bahamas). Even where solid forensic evidence is offered, conspiracy theorists quickly reduce it to bones like hungry Texas vultures.

Without a doubt, it is the most studied murder in American history. Hundreds of books have been published since 1963, and enough movies made to fill five film festivals. Along with 9/11 and Pearl Harbor, the JFK assassination is among America's most commodified and commercialized tragedies.

As a result of the frenzy, most ordinary Americans still suspect a bigger conspiracy to murder President Kennedy (76 percent in twenty-first-century polls). Put another way, only about one in four Americans think Lee Harvey Oswald was the lone gunman. But some argue the only real conspiracy has been the mercenary campaign to divert attention away from Oswald as a mediocre, frustrated little man who seized the world stage for one tragic moment.

Alas, we will likely never know whether Oswald was part of some larger conspiracy, but there's scant forensic evidence to suggest he wasn't the lone gunman that day. Most alternative theories rest on the simple assertion that Oswald couldn't have done it alone. And even if you believe there were other would-be killers in Dealey Plaza, one fact is clear: They all missed.

For the purposes of this little tour, the author assumes a) John F. Kennedy is dead, b) Lee Harvey Oswald shot at the motorcade, and c) these sites are universally acknowledged landmarks in the plot to kill the president. But, hey, it shouldn't be difficult to find alternative theories. Many conspiracy-friendly street vendors on Dealey Plaza will oblige you for a small price.

MARINA AND LEE OSWALD'S APARTMENT
The building is at 214 West Neely Street in Dallas. This is a private residence. GPS: 32.750602 / -96.825889

The Oswalds lived in an upstairs apartment and moved out seven months before the assassination. This house's backyard is where Oswald posed for his wife, Marina, on March 31, 1963, with a Communist publication and his $19.95 mail-order Mannlicher-Carcano rifle (now in the National Archives) that he would use to kill JFK, one of the most incriminating clues against him.

Oswald posed for a photo in the backyard with his rifle. STEVE RIDDLE

Conspiracy alert: Some have said the photograph was faked to frame Oswald, but modern forensic examination of the film, camera, and photos leaves no doubt the photo was taken by Marina of her husband, Lee, on that date, and it wasn't faked.

OSWALD ROOMING HOUSE

The house is at 1026 North Beckley Street in Dallas. This is a private home, but the current owner has recently opened it to paid tours to raise money for renovations. GPS: 32.755814 / -96.822814

For a month before the assassination, Oswald was living apart from Marina under the name "O. H. Lee" in this 1930s-era boardinghouse 2 miles southwest of Dealey Plaza. His $8-a-week room was barely large enough for a single bed. Police believe that after the shooting in Dealey Plaza, Oswald returned here to retrieve a hidden revolver that he used to kill Officer J. D. Tippit.

Conspiracy alert: His landlady reportedly later told investigators that a police squad car drove by slowly in those first moments after Oswald had rushed home from the assassination scene, inexplicably honked twice, and Oswald quickly left. He never returned.

RIFLE'S HIDING PLACE

The Paine House is at 2515 West Fifth Street in Irving. GPS: 32.8096678 / -96.9793331

Lee and the pregnant Marina were estranged at the time of the assassination, and she lived with Ruth Paine at this suburban home. Unknown to Mrs. Paine, Oswald hid his Mannlicher-Carcano rifle in the garage and retrieved it just before the killing.

The City of Irving recently bought the Paine House for $175,000 as a historic relic of the city's infamous past.

HOTEL TEXAS
The hotel is at 815 Main Street in Fort Worth. GPS: 32.752188 / -97.329032

JFK's last night on earth was spent in the presidential suite (Room 850) at the historic Hotel Texas, now a National Historic Landmark owned by Hilton. The last speech of his life was delivered in the hotel's Crystal Ballroom, where he was handed an envelope containing a promise of prayers from 300 local Catholic school-children. The president tucked the envelope into the inner breast pocket of his jacket. It's not known if he was still carrying it when he was shot a few hours later.

DEALEY PLAZA
In Dallas's historic West End district, where Elm, Commerce, and Houston Streets intersect. GPS: 32.778611 / -96.808333

Named for *Dallas Morning News* publisher George Bannerman Dealey (1859–1946), the parklike Dealey Plaza was created in 1936 when the so-called Triple Underpass was built to accommodate the convergence of Elm, Main, and Commerce Streets. It appears today much as it did on November 22, 1963, including many of the traffic lights. All the major buildings around the plaza existed at the time. In fact, except for a smallish granite monument (and all the conspiracy hucksters), you might not know what happened on this spot.

Kennedy's motorcade entered the plaza on Houston Street and turned sharply onto Elm just in front of the Texas School Book Depository. You might see some markings on the Elm Street pavement that denote where JFK's limo was when the shots were fired.

The assassination happened just a few yards from where Dallas founder John Neely Bryan's one-room cabin stood in 1841.

TEXAS SCHOOL BOOK DEPOSITORY

The building is at 411 Elm Street, on the northeast corner of Elm and Houston Streets in downtown Dallas. The Sixth Floor Museum is open every day except Thanksgiving and Christmas from 10:00 a.m. to 6:00 p.m. Tuesday through Sunday, noon to 6:00 p.m. Monday. Admission charged; no photography allowed. GPS: 32.779722 / -96.808333

Built in 1903, this seven-story Romanesque Revival building was erected on the site of a burned building that had been struck by lightning. Nobody knew that lightning would strike again sixty years later.

By 1963 the building was leased to the Texas School Book Depository Co., a privately held distributor of textbooks to schools

The sixth-floor window from which Lee Harvey Oswald fired the fatal shots at President Kennedy

all over the American Southwest. And one of its employees was a politically disgruntled ex-marine named Lee Harvey Oswald.

On November 22, 1963, Oswald shot President John F. Kennedy from a window on the southeast corner of the sixth floor, a storage space. After that, the floor was closed entirely for twenty-five years. The building's owner, oil millionaire D. Harold "Dry Hole" Byrd, reportedly removed the so-called Sniper's Nest window and displayed it in the banquet room of his Vassar Street mansion, where it remained until his death in 1986.

The building survived a demolition attempt and an arsonist before it was designated a National Historic Landmark in 1981. In 1989 the infamous sixth floor was converted into the 8,000-square-foot Sixth Floor Museum, which displays an amazing array of artifacts about the assassination, including oral histories, photographs, letters, and memorabilia. It is not possible to actually stand where Oswald fired his fatal shots because the window is now sealed off by Plexiglas walls. In 1994 Colonel Byrd's son loaned the notorious original window to the museum, but as with all thing JFK-related, some doubt it was the actual window where Oswald stood.

In 2000 amateur filmmaker Abraham Zapruder's family donated the copyrights to the famous Zapruder assassination film to the museum, which owns one of only three copies of the film itself. The original and the two other copies are in the National Archives.

GRASSY KNOLL
Located on the northwestern side of Dealey Plaza. GPS: 32.778805 / -96.80926

Today "grassy knoll" is an American cultural code word for "conspiracy," but until JFK was assassinated, nobody had ever used the term to describe the sloping, lawn-covered rise on the north side of Elm Street where it entered the Triple Underpass. According

The grassy knoll, which became an American code word for "conspiracy." STEVE RIDDLE

to the Sixth Floor Museum, the term was first used less than twenty minutes after the shooting by United Press International's Merriman Smith when he wrote in his first urgent dispatch: "Some of the Secret Service agents thought the gunfire was from an automatic weapon fired to the right rear of the president's car, probably from a grassy knoll to which police rushed."

Many conspiracy theorists believe the grassy knoll is the likeliest vantage point for other assassins. In 1979 the highly politicized U.S. House Select Committee on Assassinations listened to acoustic evidence from a police radio and concluded there was likely a fourth shot fired from the grassy knoll. Nonetheless, the committee concluded that Oswald's second and third shots killed Kennedy and the mysterious fourth shot from the grassy knoll missed. Who fired it? Maybe rogue Mafia or anti-Castro gunmen, the committee said, but not the U.S. or any foreign government.

PARKLAND MEMORIAL HOSPITAL

The hospital is at 5201 Harry Hines Boulevard in Dallas. GPS: 32.810278 / -96.838611

Three major players in the assassination died here. President Kennedy was pronounced dead at 1:00 p.m. on November 22, 1963, in Parkland's Trauma Room 1. Two days later, mortally wounded Lee Harvey Oswald died in Trauma Room 2. (Dr. Malcolm Perry worked on both men.) And Jack Ruby died here of a pulmonary embolism on January 3, 1967. Although the emergency room has been remodeled since the 1960s, a marker notes the three deaths.

OFFICER J. D. TIPPIT MURDER SITE

The site is on East 10th Street, between Patton and Denver Streets in Dallas. GPS: 32.747311 / -96.818456

Just forty-five minutes after the assassination, Dallas policeman J. D. Tippit, a thirty-nine-year-old father of three, stopped a man matching Oswald's description walking down the sidewalk in this quiet residential neighborhood just eight blocks from Oswald's rooming house. When Tippit emerged from his squad car, the pedestrian pulled his snub-nosed revolver and fired four shots point-blank into Tippit's forehead, temple, and chest. The shooter then walked hurriedly toward the Texas Theatre, eight blocks farther, where Oswald was eventually arrested.

Police reports say Tippit was shot 132 feet east of the southeast corner, and crime-scene photos show the spot between the driveways at 404 and 408 East 10th Street.

Conspiracy alert: Not everyone agrees that Oswald killed Tippit. Some say Tippit was part of the conspiracy, or that Tippit was actually killed by someone sent to murder Oswald. However, ballistic evidence points to Oswald as the shooter.

TEXAS THEATRE
The theater is at 231 West Jefferson Boulevard in Dallas. GPS: 32.743333 / -96.825833

Oswald sneaked into this 1931 Art Deco movie palace during a matinee of the forgettable *War Is Hell,* and employees called the cops. After a short struggle, they arrested Oswald in the darkened balcony. His exact seat was never reliably identified; it might have been any seat from the second to the fifth, according to the cops who were there.

The grand theater decayed and finally closed after a fire in 1995. While being renovated into a community performance center, all of its seats were replaced, and it's not known what became of Oswald's actual seat. Today the fifth seat from the aisle in the third row from the back is marked, but since some sections were eliminated during remodeling, the designation is more symbolic than historic.

Director Oliver Stone was permitted to remodel the theater's facade for his 1990 film, *JFK*. In 2007 an assassination documentary called *Oswald's Ghost* was the first film to be shown at the Texas Theatre since its closing.

DALLAS POLICE AND COURTS BUILDING
The official address is 106 South Harwood Street in Dallas, but the old police headquarters entrance and the entrance to the parking garage where Oswald was shot are around the corner on Main Street. GPS: 32.781709 / -96.793598

After his arrest, Oswald was brought to a holding cell on the fifth floor here, and two days later, while being transferred to the county jail, he was murdered by Jack Ruby in the basement parking garage. Today only the first two floors are used, and the general public is not allowed to visit either Oswald's old cell or the garage. But standing in front of the building, you can see the street-level garage entrance through which Ruby walked on that fateful morning.

LEE HARVEY OSWALD'S GRAVE

Shannon Rose Hill Memorial Park is at 7301 East Lancaster Avenue in Fort Worth. The grave is in Section 17 (Fairlawn) on the cemetery's western edge. Look for a small mausoleum named Shannon at the fork in the road. Oswald's nondescript flat marker is on the side of the road toward the houses, a few rows beyond a small flight of steps. GPS: 32.732376 / -97.203225

Oswald was pronounced dead at 1:07 p.m. CST—almost exactly forty-eight hours after JFK's death was pronounced. He was only twenty-four. It was the first televised murder in history, yet a whole new cover-up was about to begin. The assassin's funeral date, time, and place were kept secret to keep angry protesters away. The burial was deliberately scheduled at the same time as JFK's funeral to minimize attention.

Oswald was buried in a pine box during a funeral that cost $710. Mourners were few, so news reporters acted as his pallbearers.

Conspiracy alert: In 1981 Oswald's body was exhumed after a British author claimed a Soviet imposter was buried there. Forensic pathologists from Baylor University concluded without doubt that the body was the same man arrested for killing JFK almost twenty years before.

If you can't find the grave, don't ask cemetery workers: They've been instructed to refuse help. For years the trick was to ask for the location of Nick Beef's grave—next to Oswald's—but when the cemetery's management got wise, they stopped directing visitors to that grave, too.

Reporters acted as Oswald's pallbearers because nobody else came to his funeral.

OFFICER J. D. TIPPIT'S GRAVE

Laurel Land Memorial Park is at 6000 South R. L. Thornton Freeway in Dallas, just east of US 77. The grave is in Section 62, Lot 1, Space 7. GPS: 32.67488 / -96.81582

More than 1,500 mourners attended the funeral of J. D. Tippit (1924–1963), a Texas farmboy who became a World War II paratrooper and Dallas policeman. Like JFK and Lee Harvey Oswald, he was buried on November 25, 1963. Ironically, Tippit was not scheduled to work on the day he died, but volunteered to take a friend's shift. The initials J. D. don't stand for anything; they were his given name.

Abraham Zapruder was standing on the concrete block next to the steps when he filmed the assassination. STEVE RIDDLE

ABRAHAM ZAPRUDER'S GRAVE

Emanu-El Cemetery is at 3430 Howell Street, in Dallas, just west of US 75. The grave is in Block 52, BB East 1/2. GPS: 32.80179 / -96.79456

Dress manufacturer Abraham Zapruder (1905–1970) stood on the most westerly of two pedestals in the so-called Bryan Pergola on the grassy knoll on the north side of Elm Street (GPS: 32.779117 / -96.808907) and filmed the JFK assassination with an 8mm camera. His historic 486 frames—26.6 seconds—show the fatal bullets hitting JFK and are known as the "Zapruder film."

DETECTIVE KENNETH LYON'S GRAVE

Dallas–Fort Worth National Cemetery is at 2000 Mountain Creek Parkway, in the southwest corner of Dallas, midway

between I-20 and I-30 just off Spur 408. The grave is in Section 27, Space 308. GPS: 32.71742 / -96.94574

Korean War veteran Ken Lyon (1933–2004) was a Dallas plain-clothes detective who helped subdue and arrest Oswald at the Texas Theatre after JFK's shooting. He rode with the suspected assassin back to the police station.

SHERIFF JAMES DECKER'S GRAVE

Sparkman Hillcrest Memorial Park is at 7405 West Northwest Highway in north Dallas. Decker is in the mausoleum's Adoration wing. GPS: 32.86804 / -96.78004

Besides being Dallas County sheriff at the time of JFK's assassination, "Bill" Decker (1898–1970) also pursued Bonnie and Clyde and captured Barrow Gang member Ray "Elzie" Hamilton.

> Among the many other notables in Sparkman Hillcrest Memorial Park are baseball legend Mickey Mantle, football coach Tom Landry, and cosmetics entrepreneur Mary Kay Ash.

POLICE CHIEF JESSE CURRY'S GRAVE

Grove Hill Memorial Park is at 4118 Samuell Boulevard in Dallas, on the south side of I-30. GPS: 32.79012 / -96.72361

Chief Jesse Curry (1913–1980) drove the front car in JFK's fateful motorcade and later provided security for the newly sworn president, Lyndon Baines Johnson, aboard Air Force One. After

> Governor John Connally, who was also shot in the JFK assassination, survived his wounds. He died in 1993 and is buried in the Texas State Cemetery in Austin. (See "Texas State Cemetery," chapter 1.)

watching the Zapruder film, Curry believed JFK and Governor John Connally were hit by separate bullets and said, "We don't have any proof that Oswald fired the rifle, and never did. Nobody's yet been able to put him in the [Texas School Book Depository] with a gun in his hand." His 1969 book, *The JFK Assassination File*, fueled conspiracy fires.

DETECTIVE JOHN W. FRITZ'S GRAVE

Restland Memorial Park is at 9220 Restland Road in Richardson, just north of I-635. The grave is in Sunset Gardens Lot 30a, Space 2. GPS: 32.92554 / -96.74434

As the chief of Dallas's robbery-homicide unit, John Fritz (1896–1984) was Oswald's primary interrogator in the short time between his arrest and his killing.

Further Reading About the JFK Assassination

Publishers Weekly puts the total number of books about the JFK assassination at more than 400, and more are published every year. This paltry list should whet your appetite.

- *Best Evidence,* by David S. Lifton (MacMillan, 1980).

- *JFK and the Unspeakable: Why He Died and Why It Matters,* by James Douglass (Orbis Books, 2008).

- *Marina and Lee,* by Priscilla McMillan (Harper & Row, 1977).

- *Oswald's Game,* by Jean Davison (W. W. Norton, 1986).

- *Reclaiming History: Four Days in November: The Assassination of President John F. Kennedy,* by Vincent Bugliosi (W. W. Norton, 2007).

- *Six Seconds in Dallas,* by Josiah Thompson (Bernard Geis Associates, 1967).

- *Who's Who in the JFK Assassination: An A-to-Z Encyclopedia,* by Michael Benson (Citadel, 1998).

5

WEST TEXAS

GRAVE OF MURDER VICTIM TEX THORNTON
Amarillo

Llano Cemetery is at 2900 South Hayes Street. The grave is in Section C, Lot 117, Space 2. GPS: 35.18130 / -101.82811

Before "Hellfighter" Red Adair, there was death-defying Ward "Tex" Thornton (1891–1949). Famous for extinguishing oil-field fires with huge nitroglycerine explosions that choked off the fire's oxygen supply, Thornton was known throughout the West as the "king of the oil-well firefighters." When he struggled to put out a monster 1928 Corpus Christi fire, his wife loaded a truck with nitroglycerine and drove 700 miles to deliver it, a nerve-wracking journey that made headlines. Thornton also invented a fireproof asbestos suit and a rainmaking device to "bomb" clouds that enjoyed limited success.

But Thornton couldn't dodge death indefinitely. On June 22, 1949, the famously generous Thornton picked up a young hitchhiking couple in New Mexico. Drunk and frisky, they arrived in Amarillo, and the three checked into Cabin 18 at the Park Plaza Motel (now demolished; GPS: 35.221729 / -101.826836) near Route 66—not far from Thornton's home—for some more late-night drinking and sex. But sometime in the night, the couple beat and strangled Thornton and fled in his car. A maid found Thornton's nude body the next morning. He was fifty-seven.

A year later, killers Evald and Diana Johnson were captured, but they were only convicted of car theft, not murder. In fact, Diana

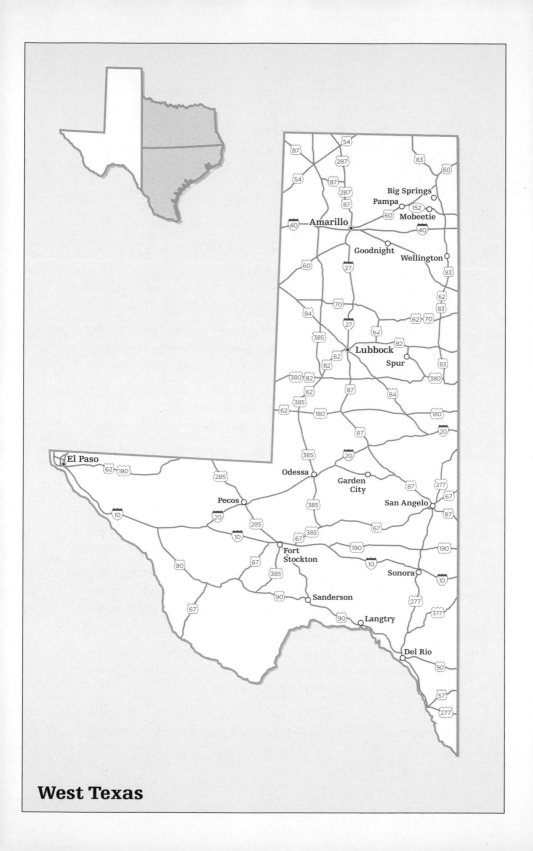

West Texas

collected the reward money for snitching on her husband—whom she promptly divorced.

John Wayne's 1969 movie *The Hellfighters* was based on the exploits of both Red Adair and Tex Thornton.

The Mystery of Killer Sostenes L'Archeveque's Grave

Here's where this book turns interactive. If you're hunting for some of the earliest outlaws in old Texas, Sostenes L'Archeveque (died 1876) is one of them . . . maybe.

The story goes like this: After his French father was killed by a white man in New Mexico, the young, half-Mexican Sostenes declared he would kill every gringo he met. And he made a good dent in his promise, killing as many as twenty-three whites before he was run out of New Mexico into the Texas Panhandle in 1876. But after L'Archeveque killed two innocent sheepherders carrying their share of a gold strike in Arizona, his own family had had enough of his evil. L'Archeveque was killed by his brother-in-law and several friends in the "robber's roost" of Tascosa (now a ghost town at GPS 35.51057 / -102.256794) and then buried on a hill overlooking the Canadian River, about a half-mile northwest of the town. For many years a wooden cross marked the spot, but it is long gone—along with the memory of L'Archeveque's exact grave site.

That's one version of the story. Another says his body was left to buzzards and coyotes. And outlaw historian Frederick Nolan has surmised that he might not have existed at all, that he was just a desperado invented to cover up crimes committed by upstanding ranchers, including the legendary Charles Goodnight.

Intrigued? You're not alone. The precise location of L'Archeveque's grave has captivated archeologists and historians for decades. If you want to mount your own expedition, you'll want to start in the remote hills of the Sierrita de la Cruz (Little Mountain of the Cross), northwest of Amarillo on FM 1061/Old Tascosa Road. The likeliest starting place would be a few hundred yards northeast of where US 385 and the train tracks intersect, on the south bank of the Canadian River (GPS: 35.52091 / -102.256622). This is private property.

BRIAN DENEKE'S MURDER SCENE
Amarillo

The International House of Pancakes parking lot is at 2100 South Western Avenue (GPS: 35.190057 / -101.884342), and the former mall parking lot is across the street (GPS: 35.189081 / -101.883398). The Western Plaza Mall was torn down in 2007, and a strip mall now sits on the crime scene.

Sporting a blue-green Mohawk, a skateboard, and a spiked collar, there was no doubt that Brian Deneke (1978–1997) was definitely a punk. And that was no easy thing in the Texas Panhandle. He sang in a punk band, promoted punk concerts, and painted whimsical road signs for pop-art eccentric Stanley Marsh III, who created Amarillo's famous roadside sculpture, *Cadillac Ranch*— ten old Cadillacs planted nose-down in a field beside I-40 (GPS: 35.187224 / -101.987117).

But not all eccentricities are well tolerated here. Friction between punks and "preps"—local jocks—had been simmering for a long time when a local high school jock named Dustin Camp and some drunken buddies barged into a local punk hangout in the IHOP parking lot looking for a late-night fight on December 12, 1997.

The ensuing rumble between fifty jocks and punks moved across the street to an empty mall parking lot. Camp jumped in his Cadillac and circled back into the crowd, crying, "I'm a ninja in my Caddy!" He drove over Deneke, crushing his head, skull, spine, pelvis, and several ribs. "I bet he liked that one!" Camp yelled as he sped away. Deneke, age nineteen, died in the snow.

Camp, then seventeen, was convicted of manslaughter in 1999 and received only ten years of probation and a suspended $10,000 fine. But he couldn't stay out of trouble and in 2001 was sent to prison for eight years for violating his probation. He was paroled in 2006.

Deneke was cremated and his ashes were scattered at a private location. His death sparked a wave of soul-searching about tolerance in Amarillo, as well as an outpouring from the punk community across the USA. Deneke's death was memorialized in the songs "Fortunes of War" by the punk-rocking Dropkick Murphys and "Brian's Song" by the Fifteens.

INFAMOUS MOLESTER'S CHILDHOOD HOME
Amarillo
The childhood home of Kenneth Parnell at 725 North Buchanan Street is now a vacant lot. GPS: 35.220417 / -101.829531

Fred Parnell abandoned his family in Amarillo during the Depression, leaving wife Mary and toddler son Kenneth to fend for themselves. Mother and son moved around a lot, renting several houses on the city's north side while Mary worked as a cook for a local cafe.

By 1940 Mary and eight-year-old Kenneth had moved to California—where Kenneth soon began a long, troubled life of sexual crimes. In 1972 he kidnapped seven-year-old Steven Stayner, whom he molested over the next seven years. When Stayner reached puberty, Parnell abducted another child, but the two boys escaped together, and Parnell was convicted of kidnapping the boys (although not their molestation). He served five years in prison but was convicted again in 2004 for offering to buy a four-year-old child for $500. He died in a California prison at age seventy-six.

The case was explored in the book *I Know My First Name Is Steven* by Mike Echols (1999, Pinnacle). Stayner died in a 1989 motorcycle accident. His younger brother, Cary, is a confessed serial killer now on California's Death Row.

JUDGE ROY BEAN'S GRAVE
Del Rio
The Whitehead Memorial Museum is at 1308 South Main Street. GPS: 29.351641 / -100.898035

The unconventional Judge Roy Bean (1825–1903) literally drank himself to death. After a wild booze binge in San Antonio, he slipped into a coma and died in his sleep in Langtry, the sleepy town he made famous. He died without ever meeting actress Lillie Langtry, whose name he emblazoned on his saloon/courthouse, but she visited Langtry in 1904, a year too late for the late judge. In that visit, Langtry was given one of Bean's pistols, which today is displayed in the Jersey Museum at St. Helier, Jersey.

Roy and his son Sam were originally buried in Del Rio's Westlawn Cemetery, but vandals caused them to be moved to the grounds of the Whitehead Memorial Museum in 1964. Bean's official Texas death certificate lists his occupation as "Law West of the Pecos."

"They couldn't bury all of him in the Del Rio cemetery," Bean biographer C. L. Sonnichsen once wrote about the judge's enduring mythology. "It seems to many, and especially to some who knew him, that the American people could find somebody better to lionize than an old rascal like Roy Bean. Perhaps so. Perhaps not. So what if Jesse James and Billy the Kid and Roy Bean were not quite what the public likes to think they were?"

Also see "Judge Roy Bean's Jersey Lilly Saloon" (Langtry).

VAL VERDE COUNTY JUDICIAL CENTER
Del Rio

The judicial center is at 100 East Broadway. GPS: 29.361352 / -100.899741

Built by the U.S. government in 1915–1916, this three-story Italian Renaissance structure originally housed the post office and federal courts. In 1995 it became the Val Verde County Judicial Center.

The most celebrated trial here was a true-crime classic: the case against sexual psychopath Tommy Lynn Sells, who might be one of the nation's most prolific serial killers. The former carnival worker and drifter crisscrossed America for more than twenty years, murdering as many as seventy people (by his own accounting) and eluding authorities who were usually left with little or no evidence. Sells's favorite targets were small children, and he especially relished multiple murders.

In 1987 Sells murdered an Illinois family who had invited him to a meal. He shot the father and then beat the pregnant mother and three-year-old son to death with a baseball bat. When the mother spontaneously gave birth to a premature fetus during her beating, Sells killed it with the bat.

On a moonless New Year's Eve 1999 in Del Rio, Sells wormed through a jimmied window and crawled into a bottom bunk bed with thirteen-year-old Katy Harris while her ten-year-old friend, Crystal Surles, slept above. Katy screamed as he molested her, so he sliced her throat with a foot-long boning knife and stabbed her

Outlaw John Wesley Hardin Sites

Few Old West outlaws rival the pure violence of John Wesley Hardin (1853–1895), probably Texas's most notable frontier gunslinger. This son of a Methodist preacher killed more than forty people, even though he spent fifteen of his forty-two years in prison. His life of crime started at age fourteen, when he stabbed a classmate for teasing him; at age fifteen, he killed his first man. Nonetheless, Hardin proclaimed all his life that he never killed anyone that didn't need killing.

Legends swirl around Hardin like a dust devil. His friendship with Wild Bill Hickok, then the sheriff of Abilene, Kansas, reportedly ended when an angry Hardin shot an innocent guest through a hotel wall for snoring too loudly. When Hickok came to arrest Hardin, the outlaw escaped on a stolen horse.

Hardin favored matching Colt .45s, which he kept in special pockets sewn into his vest or tucked into his waistband. He reputedly crossed his arms and drew his guns in one smooth motion.

In 1877 Texas Ranger John B. Armstrong captured Hardin in Florida and brought him back to Texas to face murder charges. Sentenced to twenty-five years in prison, Hardin put his time to good use: He studied law and was admitted to the Texas Bar shortly after he was pardoned in 1894. (Hardin's original pardon is in the Texas State Archives in Austin.)

Hardin opened a law practice in El Paso, but soon fell in love with the wife of his only paying client, Martin M'Rose. Some say Hardin hired local lawmen—including outlaw-turned-constable John Selman—to dispose of M'Rose, who was (unsurprisingly) killed during an arrest.

Nevertheless, on August 19, 1895, Selman spied Hardin gambling in the Acme Saloon (227 East San Antonio Avenue, or GPS 31.758285 / -106.487151). He sidled up behind the old outlaw and shot him in the back of the head. Some say Hardin's last words were "Four sixes to beat, Henry." His funeral costs of $77.50 were paid by Beulah M'Rose, the unfaithful widow of his lone (and dead) client. Repeated thefts of Hardin's headstones caused the Concordia Cemetery (see entry at right) to erect a locked fence around his grave and encase him under 4 inches of concrete. Hardin's grave is in the northeastern quadrant. GPS: 31.78087 / -106.44750

Selman (1839–1896), a former desperado who had also gunned down Texas bad man Bass Outlaw, himself was shot dead a few months later during a drunken duel with a U.S. marshal. Selman is buried not far from Hardin (GPS: 31.77954 / -106.44784).

Hardin's law office was on the second floor of the old Wells Fargo Building on the southeast corner of El Paso Street and San Antonio Avenue. Standing on the El Paso Street side (west), the office was behind the second window on the second floor (100 East San Antonio Avenue, or GPS 31.757739, -106.488849).

Three boxes of Hardin's personal papers are housed in the Southwestern Writers Collection of the Alkek Library at Texas State University–San Marcos (601 University Drive, or GPS 29.888611 / -97.943056). The papers—mostly Hardin's letters about his criminal entanglements, legal documents, and family photos—are open for research, but original material from this collection can be seen only by special permission.

at least sixteen times. As he escaped, he sliced Crystal's throat, too—but she did not die. Based on her description, Del Rio police arrested Sells for the first time in his long career as a serial killer.

Still bearing the scar on her neck, Crystal was the star witness against Sells in his 2000 murder trial here. He was convicted and now sits on Texas's death row without an execution date. He continues to confess to many other killings, has pleaded guilty to at least one more Texas child-murder, and faces charges in other states.

Also see "Victim Mary Bea Perez's Grave" (San Antonio, chapter 1).

CONCORDIA CEMETERY
El Paso
Concordia Cemetery is at 3700 East Yandell Drive, northeast of where I-10 and US 54 intersect. GPS: 31.778889 / -106.445278

- Accused of cattle rustling, Polish outlaw Martin M'Rose was a client of lawyer John Wesley Hardin. While M'Rose was a fugitive in Mexico, his wife, Beulah, and Hardin got romantic. When M'Rose finally decided to return to the United States to settle the cuckoldry, he was shot by U.S. marshals and Texas Rangers on a bridge over the Rio Grande. In his pocket was a letter to his cheating wife, pierced by two of the seven fatal shots. The only two mourners to attend his burial were Hardin and Beulah. Ironically, M'Rose is buried only a few paces from Hardin. (GPS: 31.78090 / -106.44752)

- Undercover Texas Ranger Ernest St. Leon (died 1898) was known as "Diamond Dick" because he liked to wear diamonds on his uniform. St. Leon was drummed out of the Rangers because of his alcoholism, but he remained close to legendary Ranger John Hughes. Eager to redeem himself, he helped break up a silver-theft ring and destroy a Mexican murder cartel before being rehired by the Rangers. He died after an 1898 gunfight. (GPS: 31.78099 / -106.44762)

- Shady rancher Patrick Coghlan (1822–1911) reportedly got rich by rustling cattle with his beef partner, Billy the Kid. (GPS: 31.77889 / -106.44707)

- Proving you can't choose your family (and you might be stuck with them for eternity), hanged murderer Glenn Witt (died 1916) lies next to his respected parents—both Citizens of the Republic, a Texas version of the Daughters of the American Revolution. Perhaps even more embarrassing: Witt was chased from the California murder scene by two young girls wielding hairbrushes. (GPS: 31.78002 / -106.44839)

Hardin's headstone was stolen so many times that the cemetery finally enclosed him inside an iron fence.

- Killers Antonio Flores and Geronimo Parra were hanged publicly on a day in 1900 known locally as "Black Friday" for their separate murders of a young girl and a Texas Ranger, respectively. But as they were being led to the gallows, they attacked their executioners with daggers. Jailers subdued them, and the hanging proceeded. Their families buried Parra, who was nearly decapitated by the drop, and Flores in the Catholic section of the cemetery, but their graves have never been located.

Also see "Evergreen Alameda Cemetery" (below).

EL PASO MUSEUM OF HISTORY
El Paso
The museum is at 510 North Santa Fe Drive. It is open Tuesday through Saturday from 10:00 a.m. to 5:00 p.m., Sunday noon to 5:00 p.m. Free admission. GPS: 31.759957 / -106.491597

A variety of exhibits touch—albeit tangentially—on El Paso's outlaw past. Among the artifacts are the pistol that some say killed John Wesley Hardin, some clothing belonging to the womenfolk of Teapot Dome instigator Albert B. Fall, and items related to Pancho Villa.

EVERGREEN ALAMEDA CEMETERY
El Paso
Evergreen Alameda Cemetery is at 4371 Alameda Avenue. GPS: 31.772264 / -106.440477

- Not all Texas outlaws used guns. Some, like Albert B. Fall (1861–1944), used their wits. This former U.S. senator and New Mexico Supreme Court justice was also secretary of the interior under President Warren G. Harding from 1921 to 1923. But in 1929, a few years after he resigned, he was convicted of accepting $385,000 in bribes to grant his oil friends access to naval reserves at Teapot Dome, Wyoming. The scandal was yet another blow to the public trust, rocked just a few years before by baseball's Black Sox scandal, and gave us a new slang term: "fall guy."

Fall was convicted, fined $100,000, and imprisoned for a year—the first American cabinet secretary ever to go to prison for misconduct in office. Disgraced and impoverished, he died in his sleep four days after his eighty-third birthday. Fall's two-story Classical Revival mansion (1725 Arizona Avenue, or GPS 31.775877 / -106.476758) is on Texas's list of endangered historic landmarks.

Fall's grave is in Evergreen's Section K, Lot 211, Space 2. GPS: 31.77337 / -106.44018

- Ranger-turned-killer Bass Outlaw (1854–1894) was just another figure who made it hard to tell the good guys from the bad in the Old West. Kicked out of the Texas Rangers for misbehavior, he became a U.S. marshal. During a drunken rampage at a local bordello, an old friend, Ranger Joe McKidrict, tried to calm Outlaw, but Bass fatally shot him in the face. Within moments, Outlaw was fatally wounded by Constable John Selman, who would later kill John Wesley Hardin, too. Before he died on a hooker's cot in a saloon backroom, Outlaw asked that his friends be brought to see him. Nobody came, and only a gravedigger and preacher attended his funeral. While local rumor claims he was buried in Concordia Cemetery, Outlaw was actually the third burial in Evergreen. (Section U, Plot 78, Space 1, or GPS 31.773041 / -106.43787)

- Lawyer Thomas Calloway Lea Jr. (1877–1945) made his living defending criminals, but he made his mark as mayor of El Paso during Pancho Villa's marauding activities on the Mexican border. He threatened to arrest the bandit if he ever set foot in the city, and Villa responded by putting a 1,000-peso bounty on Lea's head—dead or alive. Lea outlived Villa by twenty-two years. (Section J, Lot 33, Space 6, or GPS 31.77350 / -106.44001)

Also see "Oakwood Cemetery" (Austin, chapter 1) and "Outlaw John Wesley Hardin Sites" (El Paso).

RANGER GEORGE FRAZER'S GRAVE
Fort Stockton

East Hill Cemetery is southeast of town on Old Cemetery Road, which is east of US 285 off East Gonzales Road. GPS: 30.87595 / -102.84466

Former Texas Ranger George Frazer (1864–1896) once hired his friend Jim Miller as a deputy, but eventually their relationship became a feud when Miller became a hired assassin known as "Killer Miller." After a local hit in 1894, Frazer confronted Miller in Pecos and shot at him before Miller could fire back. Astonishingly, five bullets bounced off Miller's chest; a sixth wounded him. Miller's friends rushed him to a doctor, who removed the outlaw's trademark black frock coat and found a steel plate strapped under his shirt. When Miller recovered, he stalked Frazer and killed him.

Later, Frazer's sister held a gun on the killer, who drew his own gun and told her, "If you try to use that gun, I'll give you what your brother got! I'll shoot you right in the face!" The girl relented. Miller was eventually acquitted of murder, but just for good measure, he

Graves of Pusser Assassins

Legendary *Walking Tall* sheriff Buford Pusser (1937–1974) angered a lot of evil people with his fierce assault on moonshiners, gamblers, and racketeers in McNairy County, Tennessee. And in 1967 he paid a dear price for his beliefs when assassins ambushed him and his wife on a rural Tennessee road as they responded to a fake emergency call. Pauline Pusser, age thirty-three, was killed; a shotgun blast blew off half of Pusser's face but he survived. Pusser became obsessed with exacting vengeance on his four known ambushers—who were never formally charged in the killing.

The first ambusher to die mysteriously, Dixie Mafia hit man Gary Elbert McDaniel (1944–1969), was found floating dead in Texas's Sabine River in March 1969, shot three times with a .380 automatic pistol. His decomposing corpse was sent home to Garden City, Texas, where he was buried in the Garden City Cemetery (GPS: 31.83986 / -101.49483). Nobody was ever charged in the crime, which happened only nineteen months after Pauline's death.

Then Carl "Towhead" White, the backwoods mobster who paid for the hit, was shot to death outside a Mississippi motel the same month.

A third assassin, another Dixie Mafia triggerman named George Albert McGann (1935–1970), was murdered with a cohort in a Lubbock home in 1970. He was shot three times in the heart and head. He's buried in the Sharon Section of Trinity Memorial Park in Big Spring, Texas (GPS: 32.15836 / -101.46076). (George McGann's wife, Beverly Oliver, claimed in 1970 that she was the mysterious Babushka Lady who appears with her own movie camera in Abe Zapruder's famous JFK assassination film. It's never been proven.)

Cops suspected Pusser was involved in all three killings, but no charges were ever filed.

The fourth ambusher, Kirksey Nix, was the luckiest one. He was convicted of a 1971 Louisiana murder and sent to prison—beyond Pusser's avenging reach.

Tragically, in 1974 Pusser died in a one-car crash on the same day he signed a Hollywood contract to play himself in the sequel to 1973's *Walking Tall* (in which he had been played by Joe Don Baker). His family still believes he was murdered.

ambushed and killed the main witness against him and is suspected of fatally poisoning the judge.

Also see "Historic Oakwood Cemetery" (Fort Worth, chapter 3).

CATTLEMAN CHARLES GOODNIGHT'S GRAVE
Goodnight

Goodnight Cemetery is northwest of the town of Goodnight. From US 287, go north on Ranch Road 294 about a quarter-mile to Juliet Road, turn right and go about three-fourths mile to a dirt road on the left that leads to the cemetery. GPS: 35.04679 / -101.17467

Before Charles Goodnight (1836–1929) became the Old West's most famous cattleman, he was a Texas Ranger and Indian fighter. He's best known for guiding Rangers to the Indian camp where the famous kidnapped white woman Cynthia Ann Parker was being held and negotiating a peace treaty with her son, Quanah Parker, the last chief of the Comanches.

Goodnight and partner Oliver Loving, who developed the Goodnight-Loving cattle trail from Texas to Colorado, were brought to life as ex-Rangers Woodrow Call and Augustus McCrae in Larry McMurtry's Pulitzer Prize–winning *Lonesome Dove*. In real life as in the novel, Loving was wounded in an Indian attack and died of gangrene on the trail. Keeping a promise, Goodnight later retrieved Loving's body and brought it back to be buried at Greenwood Cemetery in Weatherford, Texas (GPS: 32.763433 / -97.792983).

JUDGE ROY BEAN'S JERSEY LILLY SALOON
Langtry
The saloon is on the grounds of the Judge Roy Bean Visitor Center on TX Loop 25. GPS: 29.809267 / -101.5604

Langtry, Texas, is really two towns. One is little more than a ghost town that's home to almost as many historical markers (seven) as citizens (fifteen), and where stray dogs and their fleas patrol gravel-and-caliche streets. Cactus encroaches from all sides, and vultures wheel in peckish circles over the occasional carcass on the edge of town. There's an ice-cream shop, a roadside museum, a few decomposing nineteenth-century buildings long past saving, and liquid southwest Texas sunsets that tint the town in sepia-shades of history. In fact, it isn't even a town at all but a decaying border colonia served by a single fire hydrant . . . with no hose.

Ah, but the other Langtry is something else entirely: a mythic place just down the road from equally mythic Deadwood and the OK Corral, where the much-fabled Judge Roy Bean dispensed "the law west of the Pecos." Bean's legend was bigger than Langtry and even the wild Pecos Country: He's been portrayed in Hollywood by

Walter Brennan and Paul Newman, and even today, you may sip a pint in the Judge Roy Bean Pub in Dublin, Ireland.

Bean was, indeed, the law. He would often fine culprits a round of drinks, or order lawyers to buy beer for Bruno, the beer-slurping black bear he kept in his saloon. Bean scribbled his own "statoots"— including the rules of poker—in a blank journal: "Cheating and horse theft," he once wrote, "is hanging offenses if ketched." Elsewhere, he noted: "A full beats a straight unless the one holding the full is not straight or is himself too full."

Once, the judge presided over the inquest of a man who had fallen to his death. After searching the corpse and finding a six-shooter plus $40, he issued his ruling: "I will have to fine this man $40 for carrying concealed weapons and that's my rulin'."

Even Langtry's name is the stuff of legend. Judge Bean was infatuated with the famous British actress Lillie Langtry, and many people still believe he named his town after her. In fact, Langtry was named for a railroad engineer who plotted the tracks through the trans-Pecos many years before Bean arrived, but that's simply not as romantic.

The Texas Department of Transportation has preserved Bean's Jersey Lilly Saloon, where he served both liquor and the law— often simultaneously. After Bean's death in 1903, the weathered-wood structure sat empty, slowly turning to dust. In 1936 the State of Texas decided the Jersey Lilly was an artifact that should be preserved, and apart from occasional fire-proofing treatments, it stands today much as it did in Bean's time.

Inside, visitors will see the single law book Bean used—or at least rested his elbow upon—when deciding his particular brand of justice. Among Bean's reputedly personal effects are his hand-cuffs, his notary seal, a walking cane, and his Victrola. There's also a pistol he supposedly seized from a corpse, and a handmade knife confiscated from one of his prisoners (although he had no jail, only a gallows).

Judge Roy Bean named his saloon/courthouse after his fantasy woman, actress Lillie Langtry, whom he never met.

Today the visitor center—which comprises the Jersey Lilly, the opera house Bean built in hopes Lillie Langtry would sing there, and a well-tended desert botanical garden—attracts about 60,000 visitors a year, most of them curious to rub up against Bean's legend.

Not only was little Langtry unable to contain Bean's legend, it also couldn't contain Bean himself. After the grizzled old judge drank himself into a coma in 1903 and died at age seventy-eight, he was buried 60 miles away in Del Rio for reasons never explained. And when vandals started visiting his grave in Del Rio's old cemetery, his bones were moved to the grounds of the Whitehead Memorial Museum, where they remain today.

Also see "Judge Roy Bean's Grave" (Del Rio).

FITZSIMMONS-MAHER PRIZEFIGHT SITE
Langtry

To reach the site from Langtry, head south on Torres Road to the bluff overlooking the Rio Grande. GPS: 29.80721 / -101.55532

Sometimes a law isn't broken but merely bent creatively. In 1896 heavyweight boxing champion "Gentleman Jim" Corbett was set to fight challenger Robert Fitzsimmons in El Paso, but Texas had outlawed prizefights. When Corbett abruptly retired, Irish fighter Peter Maher was crowned as the new champ and he quickly agreed to fight Fitzsimmons . . . but where? Ever the entrepreneur, Judge Roy Bean chartered a whole train for the fighters, boxing fans, reporters—and one Texas Ranger. In Langtry, he set up a boxing ring on the Mexico side of the Rio Grande, where Texas law couldn't interfere. It wasn't much of a show: Fitzsimmons knocked out Maher in ninety-five seconds.

The hoopla surrounding the fight caused the Texas Rangers to dispatch Ranger Bill McDonald to Langtry to keep the peace. When asked why there weren't more lawmen, McDonald replied, "Hell! Ain't I enough? There's only one prizefight!" It became the source for the motto "One riot, one Ranger."

Don't go looking for the exact spot. It's long forgotten, and the riverbank is ever-changing.

Also see "Ranger Bill McDonald's Grave" (Quanah, chapter 3).

MURDERED HOOKER MOLLIE BRENNAN'S GRAVE
Mobeetie

Old Mobeetie Cemetery is on the south side of TX 152, west of CR H. GPS: 35.50105 / -100.43864

You wouldn't know it today, but Mobeetie was once one of the toughest towns on the American frontier. Visitors, who included gunfighter Clay Allison and lawman Pat Garrett, had lots of opportunities for trouble and a big menu of saloons, like the White

Dance-hall girl Mollie Brennan might have taken a bullet for a gambler named Bat Masterson.

Elephant and Pink Pussy Cat Paradise. There was also a brothel owned by an ex-hooker named "Squirrel Tooth Alice" and her outlaw husband, Billy Thompson, little brother of "Big Ben" Thompson. And in the 1930s, bank robber "Pretty Boy" Floyd spent some time at his cousin's house in Mobeetie.

In 1876 an itinerant gambler named Bat Masterson was dealing faro at a local saloon when he was accosted by an angry soldier, Sergeant Melvin King. When King fired his first shot, a comely dance-hall girl named Mollie Brennan stepped in front of Masterson. King's first shot passed through Mollie's body and hit Masterson in the hip; Masterson then killed King. Mollie was dead and Masterson would limp for the rest of his life (although he didn't carry a cane, as the TV series suggested).

Soon after the shooting, Masterson left Mobeetie to become a deputy in Dodge City, Kansas. Former hooker Mollie was buried without fanfare in the old Mobeetie Cemetery, somewhere near a monument that was later erected in her honor. Her legacy is that she might have sacrificed her life for a man who would become one of the Old West's most intriguing figures.

Also see "Oakwood Cemetery" (Austin) and "Gunslinger Bill Thompson's Grave" (Bastrop), both in chapter 1.

MOBEETIE JAIL MUSEUM
Mobeetie

The museum is south of TX 152 at Old Mobeetie; follow the signs. Open every day except Wednesday from 1:00 to 5:00 p.m. GPS: 35.51013 / -100.44257

This is one of the few places you'll be able to see an authentic nineteenth-century hangman's machine in working order. For $1,200, it was built into this historic courthouse and jail when it

Being in jail at Fort Elliott wasn't bad . . . if the weather was nice.

was constructed in 1880. Today the old courthouse and jail are restored in a large, parklike setting, which includes an original jail cell—really just an iron cage from nearby Fort Elliott.

WHO KILLED FATHER PADDY?
Odessa

The crime scene is the former Sand and Sage Motel, now private property, at 1213 West Second Street. GPS: 31.839156 / -102.3801

The sordid tale of the Reverend Patrick Ryan's slaying in a seedy Odessa motel is the stuff of best-selling murder mysteries.

The Irish-born "Father Paddy" (1932–1981) had been assigned to a small, poor church in Denver City, Texas, after working as a missionary in Africa for twenty-five years, but he hid a secret. When he didn't show up for Christmas Mass in 1981, his tiny parish wondered where the beloved priest went. In fact, he was 80 miles south, a John Doe in the Odessa morgue. His bruised, nude body had been found in Room 126 of the Sand and Sage Motel, his hands tied behind his back and his throat crushed. There was no wallet, money, or clerical clothes in the room, just casual slacks and a golf shirt, and Ryan had rented the room with a fake name and address. Teenagers later claimed Ryan had propositioned them for sex near the motel. His truck was later found 120 miles away, missing some of his priestly possessions.

Almost a year later, an alcoholic named James Harry Reyos confessed to the priest's killing and admitted the two had sex in Father Paddy's rectory the day before the murder. He later recanted. None of the motel's physical evidence, including semen and fingerprints, could be linked to him, and the man could prove he was hundreds of miles away at the time.

But a jury ignored the evidence and convicted him on the strength of his so-called confession. He spent twenty years in

The Ghost of Betty

In some ways, Betty Jean Williams (1944–1961) of Odessa was like all seventeen-year-old girls: She yearned to be utterly unique while also being totally liked. But her uniqueness kept her from being well-liked. An aspiring actress given to dramatic flamboyance in real life, she read Kerouac and Ginsberg and fancied herself a hip intellectual. She was also sexually promiscuous long before the sexual revolution.

So when Betty began to ask people to kill her, her classmates chalked it up to her flair for drama. But Betty really wanted to die.

She finally got her wish when she convinced a popular football player and former boyfriend named Mack Herring to do it. One night, at a lonely stock pond north of town, Betty asked for a last kiss before she knelt in the dirt and held the barrel of Mack's 12-gauge shotgun to her left temple. He pulled the trigger, like she asked. Mack then dumped her weighted corpse in the pond.

Mack was eventually found innocent by reason of insanity after Betty's suicide note was read in court. It asked the jury not to blame Mack for her decision.

Betty was buried in Sunset Memorial Gardens, 6801 East Highway 80. Her grave is in Masonic Gardens, Lot 148, Space 3 (GPS: 31.88191 / -102.29900).

Legend has it that Betty's ghost still appears in the windows of Odessa High School's auditorium (1301 North Dotsy Avenue, or GPS 31.851619 / -102.383056) if you flash your headlights three times or honk and call her name. And even almost fifty years later, when something goes wrong in the school theater, somebody will say, "It must be Betty."

Before "Dog" Was a Bounty Hunter

Reality-TV bounty hunter Duane "Dog" Chapman (born 1953) has turned his violent criminal past into one of his most effective weapons. Few episodes pass without Dog telling one of his bounties about his felonious past, which is no hype: Ex–gang member Chapman has done hard time on eighteen armed robbery convictions and one murder.

In 1976 twenty-three-year-old Chapman was living with the first of his five wives and his two young sons, Duane Lee and Leland, in the alley behind a now-demolished modest house at 501 Roberta Street (GPS: 35.53597 / -100.98248) in Pampa, a Panhandle ranch town where Woody Guthrie bought his first guitar. One night, Chapman and three friends planned to steal marijuana from a pimp and drug dealer named Jerry Oliver. But after a fight broke out at Oliver's house (1072 Prairie Drive, or GPS 35.52271 / -100.96697), one of Dog's buddies killed Oliver with a sawed-off shotgun, and they all ran. Chapman was later busted in his backyard trying to evade cops. For his role in the killing, Chapman got five years in Huntsville prison but was paroled after eighteen months and returned to his native Colorado.

Although some are dubious, Chapman claims he found Jesus after his arrest in Pampa. Whether he's born-again or it's just TV make-believe, it's been more than thirty years since Chapman's last felony arrest—tempests over possibly illegal Mexican forays and angry racial slurs notwithstanding.

prison—even though the assistant prosecutor, a retired detective, and a *Dallas Morning-News* investigative reporter later claimed he was likely not the killer. Some people believe the real killer might be an unidentified but troubled man who committed suicide while waiting to give confession in an Idaho church, but Reyos's ongoing appeals for clemency have so far failed.

Ryan was buried in his native Ireland. The old Sand and Sage Motel is now Odessa's Mission Messiah women's shelter.

GUNFIGHTER CLAY ALLISON'S GRAVE
Pecos

Pecos Park is at 120 East First Street, adjacent to the West of the Pecos History Museum. GPS: 31.42703 / -103.49588

Born with a clubfoot, Robert Clay Allison (1840–1887) was the son of a Presbyterian minister, but he never let his disability or his moral upbringing get in the way of being one of the Old West's most psychotic gunslingers. At age twenty-one, he enlisted in the Confederate Army but was discharged after only a few months because of "personality" problems. He merely reenlisted with another unit, where he became a scout and a spy for General Nathan Bedford Forrest, who later founded the Ku Klux Klan.

After the war Allison moved to Texas and became a cowboy—but his mercurial temper grew even more violent. He once led a vigilante mob to lynch an accused murderer, who was beheaded by Allison himself. He was already one of the West's most feared "shootists" when he bumped into a young Dodge City deputy named Wyatt Earp in 1878, an encounter that was tense but bloodless. Nonetheless, Allison's career death count was at least fifteen men.

Ah, but Allison's ending didn't fit his gunslinger legend. He didn't go down in a blaze of glory but fell off a freight wagon he was driving. His neck was crushed by a wheel, and he later died from his injuries.

Many dead outlaws didn't get much respect at their funerals but enjoyed exalted treatment decades later when town leaders realized their ability to attract tourists. Allison was first buried in the caliche of Old Pecos Pioneer Cemetery (GPS: 31.43102 / -103.48908), but in 1975 his remains were moved two blocks to the new, lush Pecos Park, where they now rest inside an elaborate brick-and-iron enclosure beside a replica of Judge Roy Bean's Jersey Lilly Saloon.

The West of the Pecos Museum (GPS: 31.42769 / -103.49529) has an admirable collection of Old West memorabilia, but outlaw buffs will be most amused by the bullet hole near the front door, a memento of an old-fashioned gunfight at the once-nearby No. 11 Saloon.

MISS HATTIE'S BORDELLO MUSEUM
San Angelo

The old brothel is now a museum at 18½ East Concho Avenue. Afternoon tours are available for a small fee Thursday through Saturday. GPS: 31.460475 / -100.434866

From 1902 until the Texas Rangers closed it down in 1946, Miss Hattie's bordello was the most popular cathouse in the "wool capital of America." Its fame stemmed from the fact that it was connected by a tunnel to the original San Angelo National Bank a few doors east at 26 Concho, so lusty men could, um, make a withdrawal before making a deposit.

Today, Miss Hattie's Cafe and Saloon occupies the old bank building. Its dining room is decorated in plush Victorian style, and the menu offers a rich historical tour. Alas, the tunnel was long ago filled in, but the restored brothel features a lot of period furniture and interesting artifacts. Ask about the coffin.

GRAVE OF OUTLAWS BEN KILPATRICK
AND OLE HOBEK
Sanderson

Cedar Grove Cemetery is south of town on US 90, on the west side of the road. This common grave is just north of the cemetery. GPS: 30.13302 / -102.38705

Some desperadoes make history unintentionally. In March 1912 former Wild Bunch gang member Ben "The Tall Texan" Kilpatrick (1874–1912) and his buddy Ole Hobek tried to rob a Southern Pacific train the old-fashioned way: on horseback. They actually got aboard, and Hobek forced the engineer to stop the train southwest of town while Kilpatrick uncoupled the passenger cars and caboose. Kilpatrick forced his way into the mail car to rummage for cash, but while he hunted, a Wells Fargo clerk named David Trousdale whacked big Ben with a wooden ice mallet, killing him. When Hobek came back to investigate, Trousdale shot him with Kilpatrick's own rifle. The dead robbers were publicly displayed in Sanderson, then buried together in a single grave. Their botched Old West–style heist was the last of its kind in America.

Ben Kilpatrick, once a member of Black Jack Ketchum's gang, was pictured in the famous 1901 photograph of the Wild Bunch, taken in Fort Worth. He sat dead center, between Butch Cassidy and the Sundance Kid. (See "Wild Bunch Photo Studio," Fort Worth, chapter 3.)

Old West outlaw buffs might be surprised to see a small marker near the foot of the grave—the only other "active" headstone in this hardscrabble section—for Harry Tracy (1887–1944). An ill-fated Wild Bunch bandit also named Harry Tracy (1875–1902) committed suicide rather than be caught by his pursuers after a violent prison break in Oregon, and he's buried in a prison cemetery in Salem. Two

Hollywood movies were made about him. This grave (GPS: 30.13300 / -102.38701), however, belongs to a colorful local cowboy renowned for his tall tales. Maybe he knew that, someday, somebody would ask.

OUTLAW WILL CARVER'S GRAVE
Sonora
Sonora Cemetery is on the eastern edge of town, just north of I-10. GPS: 30.57929 / -100.63903

Will "News" Carver (1868–1901) started as an accidental outlaw but learned to love it. In 1895 he was wrongly accused of murdering a man, so he fled—and he stayed on the outlaw trail even after the actual murderers were convicted. After running with the Ketchum Gang and the Wild Bunch in some of the most notable frontier robberies, Carver split from his old buddies and came home to his native Texas to hide out.

Carver had enjoyed one of the wildest rides in Wild West history as a friend to notorious outlaws and a lover of shady ladies like Laura Bullion and Josie Bassett; in fact, he met his second wife, Lillie Davis, at Fannie Porter's San Antonio brothel. But on April 2, 1901, in Sonora, a posse led by Sheriff Elijah Bryant cornered Carver, who was mortally wounded in the ensuing shootout. His personal effects were auctioned off to pay his burial expenses, and Carver's mother used the rest to erect a gravestone that reads only "April 2, 1901."

Also see "Fannie Porter's Brothel" (San Antonio, chapter 1).

> Will Carver and his best friend, Ben Kilpatrick—who shared both loot and the love of outlaw prostitute Laura Bullion—both appear in John Swartz's famous 1901 photo of the Wild Bunch. Carver is standing at the back left. (See "Wild Bunch Photo Studio," Fort Worth, chapter 3.)

GRAVE OF SHOOTIST PINK HIGGINS
Spur

Spur Cemetery is less than a mile east of town on Cemetery Road, just east of TX 70. GPS: 33.47747 / -100.83798

Although his reputation never spread much beyond Texas, John Pinckney Calhoun Higgins (1851–1913) was a classic Westerner. He fought Indians, drove cattle, patrolled the range as a stock detective, ran his own ranch . . . and shot fourteen men. Some of his victims were killed in a range war known as the Horrell-Higgins Feud near Lampasas, but others were simply people who got on his venomous side. Once shown a list of his purported victims, Higgins said, "I didn't kill all them men—but then again, I got some that wasn't on the bill, so I guess it just about evens up." Unlike many gunfighters, Higgins died naturally of a heart attack while stoking his fireplace on a cold morning. He was sixty-two.

Also see "Horrell-Higgins Feud Plaque" (Lampasas, chapter 3).

ACKNOWLEDGMENTS

A book such as this requires a kind of passionate, unofficial, and unpaid support staff to point the way to the places I've described. Chief among them is my devoted wife, Mary, who rode shotgun on most of my explorations into the past. We spent our first anniversary visiting the Texas State "body farm," a grim outdoor laboratory where forensic scientists study human decomposition. When a man drags his wife to dozens of muddy cemeteries, old crime scenes, and presumably haunted buildings, and she tells him she wouldn't want to be anywhere else, then he knows he chose the right one.

Other people were also important in some small but vital ways, earning my respect and gratitude. So thank you to: Editor Erin Turner at Globe Pequot Press, my agent Gina Panettieri, Ed Allcorn, Jim Blassingame, Martin Callahan, Mike Cox, Melanie Craven, Donna Donnell, David Dawson Granade, Mary Hileman, Janet Barrett-Hobizal, Jonathan Hutson, Jan Johnson, Sherry Johnson, Stephen Joseph, Rodger and Patricia Koppa, Greg Krueger, John Manguso, David May, Donna Miers, Gretchen O'Donnell, Anita Pape, Jacob Pomrenke, John Sellars, Beverly Rogers Singleton, Julie Spence, Bebe Roper-Stewart, Troy Stone, Sarah Locklin Taylor, Cliff Teinert, Karen Thompson, Deen Underwood, Karen Valentine, Erik Vasys, and Matthew Wittmer, who often knew literally where the bodies were buried.

Thanks also to my fellow authors Chuck Convis, Rick Mattix, Claude Stanush, Steve Gabler, Steve Hodel, John Gilmore, and Bruce Barnes (son of Machine Gun Kelly), who all offered expert reflection.

Finally, thanks to all the rest who happily led me through their homes, scribbled directions, said "follow me," called other people "who should know," and shared memories that nobody ever asks about anymore.

INDEX

ABOUT THE AUTHOR

Ron Franscell is a bestselling author and journalist whose atmospheric true crime/memoir *The Darkest Night* was hailed as a direct descendant of Truman Capote's *In Cold Blood* and established him as one of the most provocative new voices in narrative nonfiction. His work has appeared in the *Washington Post*, *Chicago Sun-Times*, *San Francisco Chronicle*, *Denver Post*, *San Jose Mercury-News*, *St. Louis Post-Dispatch*, and *Milwaukee Journal-Sentinel*. *The Crime Buff's Guide to Outlaw Texas* is his fourth book. Ron grew up in Wyoming and now lives in Texas.

PHOTO BY MARY FRANSCELL